Born in 1916, Sir Owen Chadwic  ... Fellow of Trinity Hall. He is now Regiu ... History at the University of Cam ...

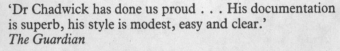

'By skilful use of diaries and lett ... and personalities to life.'
The Observer

'Better than any fiction.'
The Times

'Dr Chadwick has done us proud . . . His documentation is superb, his style is modest, easy and clear.'
The Guardian

'There can be hardly anybody who would not rejoice over the reading of such a book as this, which is quite fascinating.'
The Guardian

Owen Chadwick

Victorian Miniature

Futura
Macdonald & Co
London & Sydney

A Futura Book

First published in Great Britain in 1960 by
Hodder and Stoughton Ltd

First Futura Edition 1983
Copyright © 1960 by Owen Chadwick

ISBN 0 7088 2409 9

Reproduced, printed and bound in Great Britain by
Hazell Watson & Viney Ltd, Aylesbury, Bucks

Futura Publications
A Division of
Macdonald & Co (Publishers) Ltd
Maxwell House
74 Worship Street
London EC2A 2EN

Contents

VICTORIAN MINIATURE

Acknowledgements

I WISH to thank those who have helped me with
the loan of manuscripts or with information;
especially the Librarian of the Norwich Public
Library, Mr. P. Hepworth; Major Etienne Boileau;
Lady Harrod; Dr. John Moss and Miss Edith Moss;
Mr. Michael Balchin; Mr. Bryan Hall; Mr. and Mrs.
W. W. E. Giles; Mr. H. C. B. Philpot; Miss S. E.
Hard; Mrs. Firth; Mr. R. W. Ketton-Cremer; the
Reverend D. J. Turner, Rector of Hethersett and
Vicar of Ketteringham; and the Norfolk Record
Society.

I

SQUIRE AND PARSON

UNTIL yesterday, as it seems, the squire and the country parson were with us, the rulers of the parish in their different spheres. The manor-house would stand near the church, and sometimes the villagers, living outside the park, needed to pass through the park to their Sunday services. In its dim origins the country church had often been a chapel which the lord had founded and of which he had been proprietor. In the earliest days the distinction between the landlord's private chaplain and the vicar of the landlord's parish had been blurred. But then the lawyers recognized the parson to have such a freehold in his benefice that he could not be ejected without a court of law; and once the parson could not be dismissed, even by his landlord, there were two independent powers in the parish, and we have the relationship between squire and parson familiar to English history and the English novel.

Addison and *The Spectator* have stamped upon our minds a clear picture of the relationship: one of subservience to the squire by the parson, as though the old distinction between incumbent and nobleman's chaplain was still blurred. And indeed there were a few who, without expressing themselves with the open eloquence of Mr. Collins in *Pride and Prejudice*, would have acted as though they shared his sentiments — 'having received ordination at Easter, I have been so fortunate as to be distinguished by the patronage of the Right Honourable Lady Catherine de Bourgh, whose bounty and beneficence has preferred me to the valuable rectory of this parish, where it shall be my earnest endeavour to demean myself with grateful respect towards her Ladyship, and be ever ready to perform those rites and ceremonies which are instituted by the Church of England.' He was gratified that Lady Catherine spoke to him as she spoke to any other gentleman, and regarded her visit to the parsonage as a condescension.

Sir Roger de Coverley himself had elevated his own chaplain, as a reward for his long service, to be incumbent of his parish. The change of status seemed to make no difference to the dependence of the parson. The squire had looked for a man with 'plain sense rather than much learning, of a good aspect, a clear voice, a social temper, and if possible, a man that understood a little of backgammon'. He beautified the church with texts of his own choosing, gave each of his parishioners a hassock and prayer book to encourage them to kneel and join in the responses, employed an itinerant singing-master to instruct them in the tunes of the psalms, gave his vicar volumes of eminent preachers for use in his pulpit; and being 'landlord to the whole congregation he keeps them in very good order, and will suffer nobody to sleep in it besides himself'.

But Sir Roger was not only eccentric but old-fashioned. As he continued to wear a coat and doublet of obsolete fashion, so his notion of the squire's place in the parish church was conservative, for that place was changing even in 1711. Feuds between squire and parson, wrote Addison, were too frequent in the country and were fatal to the country people. The parish next to Sir Roger's was famous for the contentions between the parson and the squire, who lived in a perpetual state of war, the parson always preaching at the squire, and the squire, to be revenged on the parson, never coming to church. 'Matters are come to such an extremity, that the squire has not said his prayers either in public or private this half year; and that the parson threatens him, if he does not mend his manners, to pray for him in the face of the whole congregation.'

Through the legend of Sir Roger de Coverley, and through Mr. Collins, we have perhaps learnt to think that the dependence of the country parson was normal. It was not common, if the parson was neither chaplain nor curate, and for these reasons:

First, upon more than half the parishes of the country, the incumbent failed to reside. In 1827 there were 6,120 incumbents, out of 10,533 benefices returned, who were not residing upon their benefices. Some of them were holding sinecures, many of them were pluralists. The figures should be modified because some of the non-residents were clergy residing near their parish church but not in their parish. But a high proportion of the parochial work in the Church of England was performed by curates. And curates, living on pittances, unprotected by any security of tenure, liable to dismissal at a moment's notice, were inevitably servants and dependents.

Secondly, a large number of parishes possessed no resident squire, in the sense of a landlord who owned all the land and of whom all the parishioners were tenants or leaseholders. In some of these parishes the parson was the squire, or the nearest person to a squire.

Thirdly, though the squire was often the patron of the living and could appoint whom he willed, in many parishes the squire and patron were different men. The bishop was a patron, the deans and chapters were patrons, the Crown and the Lord Chancellor, the colleges of Oxford and Cambridge — the inconsequential pattern of parochial life contradicted the tidiness of squires each possessing his own advowson. Parson Woodforde had the happiest relations with the Custance family at Weston Longeville; but he had been elected to the parish by a majority of the fellows of New College, and Custance had no hand in choosing him.

And lastly, all the urban parishes must be subtracted from the list.

It is therefore probable that, even in the heyday of landowning authority, the number of parishes where the typical relationship existed between squire and parson cannot have been much more than a fairly small fraction of the parishes in the country. In that typical relationship, the squire owned all the land of the parish, except the vicar's glebe, and all the parishioners except the vicar were his tenants, whether they were farmers or bailiffs at the top of the scale or labourers at the bottom. With the ownership of the manor and the land, in this typical state which I am imagining, went the right to nominate the incumbent of the benefice.

If the squire was in any way masterful as well as devout, he ruled the spiritual as well as the secular affairs of the parish; and if an unwise parson sought to resist him, that would only mean that the church services themselves were exempt from the squire's direction and that in every other department of parochial life the parson was powerless. There is an account of a pious squire in a book of 1854, called *Ministering Children*, by

Maria Louisa Charlesworth, a book which had sold more than 276,000 copies by 1895.[1] This squire not only looked after the parishioners; he superintended the spiritual endeavours of the aged incumbent of the parish, and when he thought that the duties were being neglected, bound the old gentleman to have a curate. He selected the curate, cared about the curate's moral life, and paid the curate's salary.

But even when the vicar was appointed by the squire, the relationship was rarely one of dependence. The living was often a secure income, a stipend for a gentleman. The squire, if he held the advowson, would rarely follow Sir Roger in nominating his private chaplain. He knew more pressing claims. He had, perhaps, a younger son for whom he must provide, or a near relative, or the close friend of a near relative, as the Reverend Mark Robarts of Framley Parsonage had been educated at Harrow with Lord Lufton. If he used the advowson in the interest of his family (and he often so used it), he was nominating a gentleman of weight and substance to the parish. He would follow Sir Roger so far, that he would look for someone who was socially congenial to him and his own family, even if he did not inquire into his ability to play backgammon. To find a man whose family would be welcome in the drawing-room of the Hall, excluded all possibility of appointing a sycophant or mere dependent. If he appointed his younger son, he would leave upon his death a parish in which the squire and the parson were brothers; and younger brothers are not invariably subservient to their elder brothers.

Since the parson had a freehold in his benefice, he could resist and fight the squire without losing his income. He was the only person in the parish who could do so without fear of starvation. Where the squire was good and the parson bad, this was calamitous. Where the parson was good and the squire was bad, the parson's freehold was indispensable to his rightful influence in the parish. But in the typical parish of imagination there was quite a good squire and quite a good parson; that is to say, the squire cared for his church and his tenants, and the parson likewise. And where both men wished well to the parishioners, their friendship, as Addison knew, could be a

[1] E. Wingfield-Stratford, *The Squire and His Relations* (1956), pp. 313-14.

potent influence upon the religion, the morals, and the happiness of the people.

The wise parson took trouble to be upon good terms with his squire. It was true that his rights inside his own church were unassailable. But outside the church walls, or perhaps the churchyard gates, the squire's word was law in the parish. Everyone was his tenant or his servant, directly or indirectly. He could issue commands which were not known to the law of the land, and those commands would be obeyed. Squire Fellowes of Shotesham is said to have refused to let his tenants go into church till he came, and then to have led the congregation up the aisle; he is said to have kept a village constable to prevent them loitering when they came out again, and even in the early twentieth century the habit of gossiping at the gate after service had not revived in Shotesham.

It may be said, therefore, that the normal state of affairs contained an element of friction. Squire and parson were often the only two men of influence and substance in the parish. There might be personal antipathies, as there were with Trollope's Claverings; but where there were not, and they were friends, there would probably be a need to establish a working compromise about the parish. If both were conscientious about the parish, their spheres of influence were bound to overlap. Even into the friendliest of relationships a note of tension could enter. There was a conversation at Framley Parsonage between Mark Robarts and his wife. Lady Lufton wanted Sarah Thompson to be the schoolmistress, and was in the habit of getting her way. Was it wrong to give way, when Miss Thompson would be less effective than one of the regular trained schoolmistresses?

'If I persist this time,' said Mark, 'I shall certainly have to yield the next; and then the next may probably be more important.'

'But if it's wrong, Mark?'

'I didn't say it was wrong, Besides, if it is wrong, wrong in some infinitesimal degree, one must put up with it. Sarah Thompson is very respectable; the only question is whether she can teach.'

*   *   *   *   *

In the Victorian age the life of the deep country was changing. The tall chimneys were rising elsewhere in the land, men were making money in commerce and in manufacturing and the landed interest was declining in power. But still there were squires; still the land was parcelled into the estates of the gentry; and amid the new religious ferments of the evangelical movement and the Oxford movement, there might on occasion be more conscientious, and therefore more strenuous, differences of religion to add to the older differences of social life, or sphere of influence, or personal antipathy.

It ought to be possible for the historian to capture something of this vanished world. And yet there is an obstacle. The historian must find an articulate squire as well as an articulate parson. It is not difficult to find articulate parsons. The clergy were literate by education, were accustomed by the weekly demands upon their eloquence to express their thoughts and even their deeper feelings. Woodforde and Kilvert are celebrated, but there was a tribe of lesser diarists among the clergy. The normal squire was neither by training nor by inclination a diarist. He was often as extroverted as any farmer, improving his property, managing or mismanaging the estate, breeding his family, shooting his coverts, hunting his pack, furthering his political interest. It is possible to find articulate squires, but when we have found an articulate squire, it is not likely that we shall find him in the same parish as an articulate cleric. To illuminate that little parochial world, we need not only to know what the parson thought about a squire, or the squire thought about a parson, but how two men looked at each other across the walls, respectively, of vicarage and hall.

It so happens that at the little village of Ketteringham in Norfolk — a farm or two, a few cottages, the church and the great Hall — to attempt a description is not out of the question. The diary of the parson has survived from the Victorian age, and tells us what he thought of the squire. The diary of the squire has survived, and tells us what he thought of the parson. At various periods of their life they thought much about each other. And Ketteringham has this merit, which must have been rare enough even in that age, that the squire and the parson performed their respective duties in the parish for a long time — for thirty-one years to be exact. The parson was parson of the parish for many years longer than thirty-one; but it is more to the purpose that he was parson for the whole time that the squire was squire. The two men not only thought much about each other. They had a conveniently long time in which to think it.

Not that these two men had careers of transcendent interest or excitement. To the outside world the squire must have seemed in many ways an ordinary squire, if there was such a thing; and the parson must have seemed an ordinary parson, if there was such a thing. The squire improved his property, managed or mismanaged the estate, bred his numerous family, shot his coverts, furthered his political interest. The parson preached sermons often too long, visited the sick and the poor, educated the children, bred his numerous family, cultivated his garden, attended clerical meetings. It is true that the squire of Ketteringham was a little more than that; it is true that the parson of Ketteringham was a little more than that. But neither of them, perhaps, is of absorbing interest without the other. I do not think that a would-be biographer would be likely to want to write the squire's life, though an antiquarian might be interested in many of his activities. I do not think that the biographer would find scope for writing the parson's life, though a church historian might find instruction from his career. Apart, they are little; together, they illuminate. And together they show forth this ancient relationship between the lords, secular and spiritual, of the manor.

These two men must not be taken as typical of anything or anyone. They were their unique selves. I began by thinking, foolishly, that by describing Ketteringham I might illustrate the relationship between squires and parsons. I have ended, more wisely, by recognizing that I have illustrated fragments of the relationship between this squire and this parson.

These two men agreed whole-heartedly upon only one subject: that the Pusey ritual, as the squire sometimes called the high church innovations of his day, should be extirpated. To agree upon this, is not a little thing.

II

ANDREW

In October, 1831, Dr. Bathurst, the bishop of Norwich, received a request for ordination from a young man, aged twenty-six, named William Wayte Andrew. The bishop did not ask him why he sought ordination. That was not a question which any bishop, least of all Dr. Bathurst of Norwich, would have asked an ordinand in 1831. The bishop conceived it his duty to test the moral fitness and the intellectual quality of the candidate; he would not have rejected a man who replied that his father wished to present him to a family living. The word 'vocation' was not a word which either Dr. Bathurst or Mr. Andrew would have used.

Andrew himself was never perfectly clear what had led him to seek orders in the Church of England. He was an evangelical, believed himself a converted man, and associated this conversion with a particular time and occasion. In his first Christmas vacation from Oxford he had gone down to Cranbrook in Kent to read with Mr. Davis, the master of the grammar school. He was a fine rider; and one morning his restive hunter tried suddenly to jump a toll-gate, was prevented by the rein, put its head down and after breakneck gallop threw its rider almost through the window of a chemist's shop. Andrew was long in bed, and then on crutches, and missed the next term at Oxford; he carried the scars on his knees all his life and would have occasional nightmares of accidents on horseback. But he remembered that in bed he made a vow of dedication to the ministry. Henceforth he turned to study and not to hunting. In the long vacation a few evangelical friends came to read with him at Brixworth, his home in Northamptonshire. In term-time he would go to the evangelical churches of Oxford, St. Ebbe's to hear Bulteel or St. Giles' to hear Ball, and he began to attend the evening tea-parties of Mr. Hill, the Vice-Principal of St. Edmund Hall. Though an undergraduate of

St. Mary Hall, he took his degree. Then he went to see the venerable and saintly Mr. Jones, vicar of Creaton in Northamptonshire. Should he be ordained?

'By no means enter the clerical office,' replied Mr. Jones. Andrew was dismayed and told him how strongly he wished for it. 'Then read divinity with someone for a year,' said Mr. Jones; and Andrew had gone off to Norfolk to read with his evangelical tutor Roberts, vicar of Wood Rising. There he studied Paley and Pearson, and prayed over the ordination service.

But, in his memory, the throw from the horse seemed not to be so transforming. His memory went back, beyond the accident, to a decision to go to Oxford. In 1831, unless a man took a degree at Oxford or Cambridge, he would hardly find a bishop to look with favour upon him. Andrew had not always been destined for a university. When he was sixteen, his father had ended a prolonged course of speculation, extravagance, and misplaced trustfulness, by going bankrupt. The penniless child had been apprenticed to Mr. Castell, the draper of Gold Street, Northampton, and had spent his days moving the shutters, dusting the counters, cleaning the lamps and learning where the ribbons were kept. But first one uncle, and then another, died and left the property to him and his brother, and he was bought out of his apprenticeship. In 1826, his father died after a crash in a carriage which he was driving while intoxicated; and three months later Andrew attended the election at Northampton.[1] Being ignorant of the difference between Whig and Tory, he joined Mr. Whiting's party and listened to the speeches delivered from the balcony of the George Hotel. The party of Sir George Robinson pulled up pavements and smashed the windows of the hotel, and Andrew found himself escaping from flying stones into All Saints' church and hiding under the organ. When he emerged, he joined Mr. Whiting and Sir John Ross (the navigator) and a few others and walked arm-in-arm past Northampton gaol.

[1] The Northampton election of 1826 is of some constitutional importance. It was the election when the Tory majority in the Corporation voted £1,000 to defray the expenses of their unsuccessful candidate, and the right to do so was challenged in Parliament.

Whiting said, 'What do you think of Mr. Whitworth's speech? He has been to the university; why don't you go?'

In Andrew's memory the question was like a thunderclap. He remembered leaning against the iron railing in front of the gaol, and then ordering his horse and riding home to his mother to tell her, 'I shall go to the university!' He had decided to be a gentleman, and to learn how to speak in public like Mr. Whitworth.

One morning he set off after breakfast and rode the fifty miles to Oxford, laming his horse on the way, to see what could be done. In Oxford he recollected that at a shoot near Melton Mowbray he had met Dr. Dean, the principal of St. Mary Hall, and after a day or two called upon him. He told Dr. Dean that he thought of entering the university. Andrew, who had left school aged fifteen and a half, knew little Latin and no Greek. Dr. Dean replied that he would have difficulty in securing entrance to a college. Then he added, 'If you like to come here, we will receive you.' Andrew, happy in his ignorance, said at once, 'I'll come.' He took his rooms, ordered his cap and gown, and sent to Brixworth for his portmanteau. Before long he was walking down the High Street in a silk gown and velvet cap, covering a grass-green short riding-coat with bright brass buttons, a buff waistcoat, white breeches, and top boots.

St. Mary Hall was not altogether suitable as a place of residence for a young man who fell off a bolting horse and afterwards devoted himself to prepare for the ministry. In 1829 there were twenty-six undergraduates in residence. They were all wealthy, kept their bells and livery servants, ordered more dishes at table than there were men to eat them, were permitted to keep their hunters and attend chapel with top boots and pink under their gowns. It seemed the most expensive place of residence in the university. Dr. Dean was a good scholar, and an amiable and benevolent man. His conversation was larded with classical allusions and clever quotations, he had a fund of anecdote and a keen relish for the ridiculous, he amused a large circle of friends. He was not, we are told, a provident man, and his financial embarrassments were increased by the clamours and importunities of needy and not over-scrupulous relatives. The finances of St. Mary Hall were not wholly free from embarrassment, and to one critic it appeared like a sort of tumbledown hotel[1]. Evidently, Dr. Dean was a warm-hearted cleric of the old school, and it is intelligible that a rather puritanical under-graduate, reacting against a drunken and bankrupt father, should have distrusted him. Andrew thought Dr. Dean intemperate; he thought the vice-principal to be the same. Looking back, Andrew could not think that the university of Oxford had contributed significantly to his preparation for the ministry, except by allowing him to read for ten or twelve hours a day and by directing him to Mr. Roberts of Wood Rising.

If he was to persuade a bishop to ordain him, he must find a title to which he might be ordained. There were two discouraging starts — the first because the prospective vicar refused to have so evangelical a curate, and the second because Dr. Bathurst, the bishop of Norwich, thrust him away at the interview.

Dr. Bathurst was not popular with his clergy. He was already eighty-seven years old, and incapable of discharging effectively, sometimes of discharging at all, the duties of a large diocese. In his old age he needed to spend every winter at Bath, and was therefore absent for many months from his diocese. He was also a Whig, who had voted for Roman Catholic emancipation and would vote for the Reform Bill and was widely believed to be an Iscariot. He distressed some in his diocese by courteously taking off his hat to recognize dissenting ministers in the streets of Norwich. He was also notorious for playing cards — that is to say, he was accustomed to solace the loneliness of his evening hours by playing whist with three ancient ladies. There was once a public (but erroneous) report that the archbishop of Canterbury had been requested by the bishop of Chester to admonish the bishop of Norwich upon the subject of whist. Neither his public nor his private character attracted the more strict, or the more Tory, among his clergy. His biography, published by his daughter in 1853, did nothing to destroy the impression that the bishop was an anachronism from the eighteenth century.

Andrew resented the interview. The bishop conducted an unusual inquiry. Instead of examining the prospective curate,

[1] Notes by Philip Bliss (Oriel College Muniments S. II. K. fo. 242), a reference which I owe to the kindness of Mr. W. A. Pantin; *Memorials of Bishop Hampden*, p. 92.

he appeared to Andrew to be seizing the opportunity to investigate the life of the prospective rector. Andrew refused to answer these personal questions about his intended employer. The bishop rose from his seat in anger and said, 'You don't know what you come for, sir!', and dismissed him.

A few weeks later Roberts of Wood Rising invited Andrew to visit the coast with him. They rode to Cromer, a place which disgusted them, and thence to Mundesley. On the way back, at the cross-roads by Gimingham, Roberts stopped his horse and said, 'Shall we call on the curate here?' 'As you please,' said Andrew. Roberts left Andrew at the cross-roads and found the curate, Sharpe by name, in distress. He had just been offered the living of Cromer, with about £90 a year. His present stipend as curate of Gimingham was £100 a year. If he left Gimingham, no evangelical would succeed him and 'the Gospel would cease'. But if he retained both Gimingham and Cromer in plurality, he would be legally bound to provide a curate for Cromer and would be unable to afford the legal stipend. Therefore he felt himself obliged, though reluctant, to refuse to accept the living of Cromer.

Roberts arrived back at the cross-roads, and said, 'Andrew, here is a call from God to you.' For Andrew had money and would need no stipend. 'What! I go to a place of 1,200 souls and that a fashionable resort, with such a cathedral church?'

After a few days he came to think that this was a call. He sought letters of testimonial from three beneficed clergy; but one of them signed that he had known Andrew less than two years, and Dr. Bathurst refused to accept them. He sent the papers with all speed to Northamptonshire, and a messenger secured the signature of old Mr. Jones as he descended from the pulpit of Creaton church.

*   *   *   *   *

The time of examination was a time of trial. Both his intended vicar and himself had offended the bishop. 'You must be very careful,' said Mr. Sharpe, 'for I tell you, his Lordship will prevent your ordination if possible.' Andrew afterwards attributed his success to a providential circumstance.

The day before the first examination (he was staying in Norwich at the Bowling Green Inn) he walked with Roberts to present his testimonials at the registrar's office. By chance they met Mr. Newton, agent to a friend of Andrew.[1] When he learnt that Andrew had come to Norwich for the purpose of being examined for orders, he said, 'I know the chaplain. He is a friend of mine. If Mr. Andrew will breakfast with me in the morning I will introduce him.' He went to breakfast next morning and was introduced to the bishop's chaplain. So 'the questions of that day passed off agreeably'; though Andrew thought it a pity that he was asked scarcely a question out of Pearson, to which he had devoted so much time. The next morning he returned to the palace and wrote an English and a Latin theme. This completed the examination, and he must now go before the bishop. He was not encouraged when at the very doorway to the bishop's apartments one of his predecessors cried to him, 'Goodbye to you. I am plucked.'

Andrew felt alarmed, and was yet more perturbed when he observed that the moment he entered the room the bishop rose and left it. The chaplain said, 'Mr. Andrew, the bishop does not like your Latin theme.' Andrew's suspicion of prejudice rose in his mind. He knew that his Latin composition had gained him his degree at Oxford.

'What part, sir, is objectionable? Is it grammatical?'

'Yes,' said the chaplain, 'but . . . his Lordship objects to it.'

After a little argument the chaplain allowed him to write another. He prayed over almost every word. As he was going to present it he knelt down at the step of the door and begged grace that he might be resigned if this was the Lord's way of hindering him from following a wrong path, and that he might be contented to spend his days as a layman.

The chaplain (Mr. Drake) received the copy of the second theme. He said, 'Mr. Andrew, will you write a piece of Latin in my presence?' 'Certainly, sir.' He was given the passage beginning 'What went ye out into the wilderness to see?'

The chaplain eyed the result for a moment, and said, 'That will do very well, sir. You will present yourself for ordination tomorrow.'

[1] The friend was Mr. Weyland of Wood Rising, the father of the Poor Law reformer whose biography is in the *Dictionary of National Biography*.

That afternoon Andrew spent sweet moments in a summer-house at the corner of the bowling green.

The next morning he went to the palace and assembled with the other ordinands in a large room. The old bishop entered leaning on the arm of Mr. Kitson, the registrar, and saying, 'What a fool the man was!' Andrew tried to find quiet before the service by walking in the cloisters, but was disturbed by the levity of some of the men to be ordained with him. Even during the service he disliked the irreverence and tittering from some of his fellow-candidates. After the service several of the others went to the Maid's Head to eat a good dinner. Andrew went not to the Bowling Green Inn, but to a field about a mile on the road to Dereham, and there found joy and sweet communion, and over and over again renewed the dedication of himself.

*   *   *   *   *

Mr. Sharpe, who had been curate of Gimingham for fourteen years and was now vicar of Cromer also, was four and a half feet tall with a head disproportionately large; his wife topped a comfortable six feet. Sharpe had but one eye and that already beginning to lose its sight. He preached standing on a stool, with his notes held high to the eye. He came in time to command Andrew's deep respect. The curate, though he lived and ministered during the week at Cromer, was required to conduct the Sunday services at Gimingham.

As yet he had found no lodging in Cromer. He took a whole house at a rent of £25 a year and hired a housekeeper and a lad from the village of Scoulton. He found to his surprise that living in a house nearby was a man named Hanbury whom he had known as an undergraduate at St. Mary Hall. Hanbury, a cousin of the Buxton family, had left the university without a degree and taken rooms in Cromer in order to read under the tuition of Mr. Sharpe. 'Ah, poor fellow,' mused Andrew, 'he is hoping through interest to be ordained without a degree.' He did not rate highly Hanbury's fitness of mind, body, or spirit for ordination.

The instant he settled in Cromer, invitations to dinner began to pour in. He consulted Sharpe, who told him to be cautious. He characteristically determined to refuse them all. He could not accept them all, and if he accepted some, he would offend those whom he refused. He had a qualm that the decision might be puritanical, but rejected it. The decision was to be momentous later in his life.

His conduct as curate was sometimes marked more by the harmlessness of the dove than by the wisdom of the serpent. Three young prostitutes came one Wednesday to the meeting for girls, for the purpose, he supposed, of having some fun. The second time they came he had to rebuke them for exciting laughter. The third or fourth week he threatened two of them with exclusion and they came no more. But he saw that the third, Elizabeth Jacobs, had become more thoughtful and she remained with the class until he began to employ her in his house when he wanted extra help. Then he took her into the house for a month as a servant, and later employed her as a maid.

Upon another occasion he achieved a measure of unpopularity by boldness with Mrs. Heath, the dying wife of the chemist. Her husband would allow no one to see her, not even Mr. Sharpe. Andrew determined to get to her bedside. He called at the house and inquired of the husband. After some talk he asked if he might see her. Heath hesitated, but gave way. As Andrew was climbing the stairs, Heath said to him from behind, 'I hope, sir, you will not say anything to make her unhappy. She is fully aware of her state and of all good things.'

Andrew replied, 'Mr. Heath, you are little aware of a minister's serious responsibility. I must speak about her soul, but it shall be very mildly and in few words.'

He spoke gently as he supposed, and kept the time short because he wanted to be allowed to come again the next day; particularly because Mrs. Heath expressed a wish that he should. She died in the night or next morning; and while the church bell tolled for her soul, it was rumoured in the town that Andrew had hastened her death by harsh and painful questions.

But for the most part Andrew was not unpopular. The children of Cromer loved him. They would crowd round him, trying to clasp his hand; and when he arrived from a visit to Brixworth, bringing his young sister Laura to stay with him, they stripped the fields of flowers to greet his coach as it came into the town. They ran after the coach and forced him and

Laura to dismount and walk with them. Everyone started looking out of their windows, and Andrew feared that some would be envious of the children's affection for him. He turned off the road and entered his house by the back lane.

Meanwhile, he was preparing for priest's orders. His preparation consisted of writing themes for the eye of Mr. Sharpe. When he went to Norwich for his examination and heard the subject given out, he remembered that he had written a theme on that very subject only a few weeks before. Putting his hand in his pocket he pulled out a paper and found it to be the very one. His examination therefore consisted simply in copying down his old theme on the piece of blank paper which he had been given. 'How many such singular providences have I met with in my short life!' After the ordination in the cathedral, he walked straight over to St. Simon's church to preach a sermon.

Now that he was a priest, the bishop insisted that Sharpe reside in Cromer. Sharpe and he therefore exchanged parishes and houses. He was still Sharpe's curate; but Sharpe now shepherded Cromer and Andrew, Gimingham.

'Tis written, 'he that exalteth himself shall be abased,' which may account for this gloomy day. I inwardly exalted that my Sunday scholars had made such progress under my care; but having invited a party of gentry to witness the examination, how was I mortified to find that when Mr. Sharpe stood up to catechise, the children could not answer a single question. In vain did I urge or seem displeased; it was quite a failure. I knew not how to apologise, for the matter was unaccountable, the children were dumb. But this evening the mystery is revealed. A few parents, viewing my manifest grief, came to say that the children never could answer a question to Mr. Sharpe, his manner is so harsh; they could answer all to me. This trial may be useful to me not to seek the praise of men, but that which is of God only.

The charge of the lambs of the flock is most interesting but oft-times most difficult and discouraging. Report has now reached me that a band of boys and girls meet at a house for the most indecent and immoral practices . . . I have adopted this plan. Having learnt the parties, I went to the first, and after some serious and affectionate conversation said I feared she was not going on as months past. She confessed it. I then gave her credit for being led away by others and obtained her assurance that she would not associate with the one I mentioned. I then proceeded to this one and urged most strongly her danger if she kept company with the former one, and so on through the whole party; till I found I had set every man's hands against his fellow. I returned home to ask the Lord to bless the wisdom I trust His Spirit inspired me with.

I have been to my dear flock not only a sentinel to give alarm by day but a watchman by night, frequently parading from one end of the village to the other almost at all hours; so much so that the dear children fear even to go on errands for their parents after dusk, saying, 'I know, mother, I shall see Mr. Andrew round some corner.' I feel daily the importance of these nightly ambulations, and the dear children dread losing my love by being about at a late hour. I have often had encounters. The other evening I saw a tall Anakim-looking man casting stones in fun at a servant who seemed much annoyed. I reasoned with him and begged him to throw down the stone he held. He refused; and turning on his heel said he was not going to stand to be talked to. At this my courage rose; and I laid my hand on his shoulder, and in somewhat of an authoritative tone exclaimed, 'I defy you to stir! I have a message from God to you and you must hear it.' The man appeared as one petrified; and after my message he threw down the stone and walked away very quietly. It is somewhat strange I never could learn who the man was though I oft wished to know the effect. God, I thank Thee for this opportunity of being valiant for Thy truth, but never let me lack wisdom (and in a later hand he has added 'which now in after years I feel I did').

* * * * *

The question of matrimony had now become urgent. Long ago in childhood, he remembered, he had been taught by a superstitious maidservant to lay his shoes in the form of a cross on Good Friday night so that in a dream he might see his future wife. But he had never thought seriously of marriage, being indeed too busy. He found that the unmarried state was inconvenient to his work. There were homes which he could not enter. Sharpe would not allow him to visit young females, even on their death-beds, except in exceptional circumstances. A young lady whom he helped by his ministry was persecuted by her family for being religious. Andrew could not offer her the care and comfort which he felt her to need. There were at least two other cases of a similar kind. He could not help saying to himself, 'What liberty in this respect you would have as a married man!' He found that the gossip of the village had already married him to a Miss Ives from Mundesley who frequently attended his church with her widowed mother. When he heard the rumour he smiled to himself. 'I do indeed love her soul, but I have never thought about her body.'

As the practical difficulty pressed upon him, he became convinced that he must marry for the sake of the liberty of his ministry. For a few weeks he placed at the centre of his devotions that he should be directed to the right person. It was his custom in private prayer to prostrate himself at full length before the altar in the church, or kneel at the reading-desk with hands aloft. Sometimes he would walk out along the beach and pray in the cleft of a rock to the thunder of the breakers. There was a laurel bush growing in his garden, which seemed numinous, consecrated. His morning prayers were always said in a dark northward-facing attic of the house; and in some moods his house would seem to him a house of prayer, more like a church than a private dwelling; even the stairs reminded him of the moment when one midnight he had knelt upon them to pray for the life of a servant whose illness was alarming. In the last months of 1833, these times of prayer turned towards the choice of a wife.

He looked among his acquaintances and found that four young ladies were possible. We do not know the criterion by which the four were selected, nor do we know the names of all four. One of them was Miss Ives; one was Miss Upcher; a third was Miss Ellen Wickes, the daughter of a devout layman who lived at Aylsham. One morning when he was saying his prayers by the laurel bush, the name of Ellen Wickes came into his mind with an extraordinary sensation. He rejected it. He remembered that she was almost a stranger. But during the day he kept thinking of her, willy nilly. His studies were interrupted by the recollection, and that night he could not sleep. In the morning he determined no longer to resist, but to make secret inquiries about her.

He first told his mother, who was surprised but arranged the required opportunity. She invited Mr. and Mrs. Wickes and their daughter to Gimingham for the children's frolic. Though Miss Ives was also at the frolic, the day confirmed Andrew in his conviction that Ellen Wickes should be his bride. Thenceforth he took her name daily to his prostration before the altar.

When his mother and Laura were due to return to Northamptonshire, they were invited to spend the evening at Aylsham, on their way. Andrew went with them. Next morning he rose very early and retreated to the summer-house to prepare himself for the 'conflict' of the day before him. At the end of lunch he asked Mrs. Wickes if he might have a few words with her. They retired into the drawing-room and sat side by side upon the sofa.

'You perhaps will be surprised at my question. Is your daughter Ellen engaged?'

'No,' said Mrs. Wickes hastily.

'I am convinced that it is for God's glory that I should become a married man. I have made it a subject of earnest prayer and I seem to have been directed to your house. I shall therefore consider your answer the answer of God.'

She said with some confusion, 'You must mention it to Ellen herself, but I will call Mr. Wickes.'

Wickes ('poor old gentleman' thought Andrew), when he heard the question, grasped his hand and broke down in sobs and tears. Andrew then advanced 'with calm and prayerful steps' to the study, and spoke to Ellen in similar words. She trembled and began to weep; and then begged a short time for prayer. The next morning they read together a chapter of St. John's Epistle; and a few days after Andrew's return to Gimingham, he received the letter of assent. He believed that he had been led to her almost by inspiration. He gave her a brooch. Once in childhood an artist had come from London to his village, and his father had refused to be painted. The child had sat in Finedon church to be painted instead of his father; and the resulting miniature was framed in a brooch which Ellen Wickes would wear for the rest of her life.

During his engagement he made a habit of riding over to Aylsham every Monday evening and returning to his parish on Tuesday morning. But these visits were interrupted, in the first months of 1834, by the need to keep a period of residence at Oxford as a qualification for taking the degree of M.A. — 'the Master's term' as he called it. He now regretted that he had not kept the residence before his engagement. Part of the time at

Oxford he was confined to his house with an excruciating toothache, and otherwise he spent his leisure in copying the texts to which Bunyan refers in *Pilgrim's Progress*. He dined in St. Mary Hall, where the Principal was now Dr. Hampden. He was delighted when he was asked by the junior men to say grace. He thought that the request would have been ridiculed in his own time three years before, and attributed the improvement to the new Principal's care for the morals of his men.

Early in March he returned to Gimingham and on 18th March, 1834, was married at Aylsham church. Hymns were sung at the marriage feast. As the bride and bridegroom drove away in their carriage, her brother galloped after them and gave them the keys of all their luggage. They went through Cambridge to Oxford, where he took the degree of M.A. Thence they went for a short visit to North Wales and Anglesey. After travelling all night they arrived in Chester at 6 a.m. on Good Friday and fell asleep on the sofa until the time for service at the cathedral. During the service he several times fell asleep while standing up and caught himself falling. They arrived back at Gimingham on the Tuesday after Easter. His household had changed by reason of his new consequence as a married man. He had two horses instead of a pony, and a gig with a servant in livery. His housekeeper, Susannah Beets, had left to become a schoolmistress.

His early married life was marked by a strange incident. A friend came uninvited to spend a few days and conducted one of the services on Sunday most irreverently.

About midnight Andrew and his wife were wakened by a reverberating crash. Ellen exclaimed, 'H. is dead!' Andrew leapt out of bed, and found his way through the darkness along the landing to the door of the visitors' bedroom. Outside the door he waited, listening. There was no sound from within. Andrew was convinced that Ellen was right and that H. was dead. He dare not enter the room but knelt down upon the floor of the landing and began to say his prayers for mercy upon H. Then he called aloud for H.'s servant, who at first would not be roused, but at last came groping along the passage. Suddenly the servant was heard filling the night with groans, and Ellen and Andrew were confirmed that H. must have fallen dead. Andrew rushed again at the bedroom door, and discovered that the servant had mistaken the door of the bedroom, groped his way inside a closet instead and hurt himself. Andrew helped to extricate the servant and together they entered the visitor's bedroom. H. was fast asleep in bed. They lit a candle, and found a large mahogany table crushed to pieces in the centre of the room. H. had placed on this table his heavy writing-desk and other belongings, had climbed out of bed in the dark and knocked the table over (perhaps in a fit to which he was liable) and hastily climbed back into bed to feign sleep and avert discovery. Andrew taxed him, but he would confess nothing. In the morning Andrew told him that he could not ask him to spend another night in the house, particularly as 'the consequences might be most serious for Ellen in her present state'.

The same year Andrew left Gimingham. The rector, Mr. Blakelock, had decided to reside and no longer needed his curate. They were already packing before they had found anywhere to go. Ellen, big with child, perhaps minded the sense of insecurity more than her husband. But they had friends who found them, just in time, the curacy of Witchingham, where also the vicar, Dr. Jeans, was not residing. When they drove out of Gimingham in the carriage of Mrs. Wickes, a crowd of villagers gathered to wave them farewell. They left the problem that Sharpe could not afford to be vicar of Cromer without the pay of the Gimingham curacy. Andrew solved it by collecting about £70 from his friends every year thenceforward and presenting it to Sharpe.

*   *   *   *   *

'What a change! I have exchanged a people among whom the Gospel has sounded loudly for fourteen years, for another who scarcely know the meaning of the term; for I can't learn that the magnificent temple has ever sounded with the tidings of salvation except from the desk. The Methodists perhaps have preserved the people from heathenism.'

His reputation for earnestness had preceded him. The previous curate, Mr. Reynolds, refused to allow his furniture into the house, and one of the leading citizens refused to do any repairs. At first they could extract no water from their pump and had to bring every drop from a farmhouse. The squire and his lady, Mr. and Mrs. Tompson, however, were not offended when Andrew and his wife refused their invitation to dinner, and later came to a tea at the curate's house and an evening of Bible reading. Their daughters afterwards became district visitors in the parish. Though the church and house stood two miles away from most of the inhabitants, and though the church was a miniature cathedral in size, Andrew soon found that his people came flocking to receive his ministrations, sometimes crowding not only the aisles but even a kind of bell-chamber near the roof. He disliked some of the customs which he found to prevail. It reminded him how his old tutor in Kent, Mr. Davis of Cranbrook school, used to arrange that several people should remain behind after the sacrament to join in consuming the consecrated wine. He found at Witchingham a custom of distributing the alms the moment the sacrament was over. His clerk shocked him by saying, while the congregation were departing from the sacramental table, 'Please sir, Mr. Reynolds always gives me a shilling.'

At Witchingham, Ellen's time came for the birth of the child. Her labour began on the night of Saturday, 17th January, 1835. The groom, Peter, was sent four miles to Reepham to fetch Dr. Wordingham. The doctor was a strange man, about sixty years old and with rough features, wearing top boots, two great-coats, and a handkerchief tied up to his nose. He spoke in what Andrew thought to be a surly tone of voice; and instead of bending over the bed of travail where Ellen was moaning, he stood warming his back at the bedroom fire, saying, 'Come! there's no cause for so much noise.' 'Nurse,' he said, 'can't you put me into a bed? I shan't be wanted yet.' The nurse showed him her own bedroom, where he covered his head with her cap and fell asleep.

When the pains began to increase, Andrew could no longer bear to remain in the bedroom, and went down to the dining-room. But there he could still hear the cries upstairs; and though he walked out into the garden and then into the next field to escape the sound, he could still hear it. It was now Sunday morning and the church bells began to ring. He trembled at the thought of going back to the house to put on his gown for the service, but all was mercifully silent upstairs whilst he made himself ready. As he read morning prayer in church he kept fancying that he could hear groans. In the midst

of his devotions at the end of morning prayer, the clerk inter-
ruped him, saying, 'Please, sir, there's a woman to be churched!'
Andrew felt this was too much; but he faltered through the
service of churching.

While the congregation was singing he walked towards the
altar. As he passed his pew he saw his maid Emily, who had
just come into church. Her eyes were streaming with tears. He
leaned over and whispered to Emily, 'How is she?' Emily's reply
he could not catch; he thought she said, 'All things are as they
were.' But he was not sure that he had heard aright; and when
he returned to his reading-desk she whispered distinctly, 'All's
well, a fine son and heir!' Andrew's heart leapt and, going up
into the pulpit, he preached a sermon from the text which
Ellen had long ago chosen for the occasion, Isa. xliii. 2: 'When
thou passest through the waters, I will be with thee; and
through the rivers, they shall not overflow thee: when thou
walkest through the fire, thou shalt not be burned. . . .' It
seemed to the preacher, however, that the congregation was not
attentive. They looked more at each other than the pulpit.

At the end of the service he hurried into the house, but could
not bring himself to enter the bedroom. He felt that his own
emotions would break out and that she must be kept calm. He
thought that he had better ride off to the other church, take
service there, and hope that he would be more collected when
he came back. But the moment he entered the dining-room he
was told that Ellen must see him directly. He summoned all his
courage to dare to see the little babe at the breast.

*   *   *   *   *

Poor Mrs. H(oward) how I pity you! She has bounced out of my
church in rage and by Miss C's report it may be doubtful whether
she may not (as many do) take revenge on me by abstaining from
ordinances and starving her poor soul. And for what! because her
minister positively asserted that she and the rest of mankind were
born in sin and deserved eternal wrath the instant we were brought
into the world . . .

On 20th April, 1835, being Easter Monday, about noon, a
man with a drawn sword entered the yard of the house,
followed by a band in marching order. It was the Friendly

Club. Andrew was grieved to see in the band men of whom he had hoped for better things. They had come to ask for a contribution. He said that he would come down to the village that evening, and if he found them quiet he would give them something. After sending the servants to bed, he and his wife drove down to the village in the gig. They found stalls erected, people shouting and children crying, while at the lower room of the public house was drinking and singing and in the upper music and dancing.

Andrew took a stance with folded arms in the front room of the public house. He heard a whisper running round the room, 'There's Mr. Andrew!' He called to the constable and said, 'Go through the house and see who is there.' The effects were magical. The dancing ceased, the band stopped playing, the singing died away, and slowly the people drifted to bed. Next morning he went down again to the village and found everyone gossiping of the night. 'The constable declared he never had such a feast. For years he was accustomed to be up nearly the whole week and oft narrowly escaped with his life; but he was never requested this year but once.'

Visited Mrs. Thorn: found her in a bedroom to which she has been confined for years. The room was about fourteen feet square, contained a very nice bed and furniture. On one side of a large fire sat her wealthy husband, and her companion in the front. Four or five cats were on the bed, which it was treason to touch except for the purpose of caressing. Two or three others lay on the hearthrug and a huge greyhound extended at full length on the sofa; and I may add that the least sagacious of the party lived with as great seeming consciousness of a future state as their afflicted possessor. Religion was considered a strange thing, her husband always did 'all he could', never did any harm etc. and the companion assented to everything advanced. Having been forced to taste her cake and wine we with great discouragement and disgustful pity took our leave.

The use of 'we' in the last sentence was probably a meaningful plural. Ellen went visiting with him whenever she could.

*　　　*　　　*　　　*　　　*

Towards the end of 1835, Dr. Jeans, the non-resident vicar of Witchingham, died; and again the Andrews found themselves in imminent danger of being without parish or home. The patrons of the living were the Warden and Fellows of New College, Oxford. Two of the Fellows came down to Witchingham in succession to view the prospect for themselves. Andrew liked the second better than the first, but if either accepted the living, he was pessimistic about the religious future of the parish.

He and his wife went to stay at Aylsham, where Ellen's father had died a few weeks before. Andrew was digging in the upper garden when a servant came from the house to say that a gentleman was waiting to see him. He went into the house and found that the gentleman had gone but had left a parcel. Ellen and he went into the drawing-room. Mrs. Wickes thrust the parcel into Ellen's hand saying, 'Accept that with my love,' and left them wondering. They opened the parcel and found a presentation to the living of Ketteringham.

Neither of them knew where Ketteringham was. They asked Mrs. Wickes. She desired them not to ask any questions but to accept it as a call, and Andrew thought that this was right.

The farewell services at Great and Little Witchingham, like that at Gimingham, were attended by crowds. At Little Witchingham he was obliged to have the surplice handed over the heads of the congregation from the communion table. As they walked down the aisle Mrs. Howard, who a few months before had bounced out of the church in a rage, pressed through the throng and seized Ellen's hand, silently weeping. From the church the people formed a path between two lines, and the Andrews hurried through them, handkerchiefs pressed to their eyes. The crowds followed them across the fields.

During his first months at Ketteringham he was comforted because some of the Witchingham folk would travel the sixteen miles to Ketteringham to continue hearing his sermons.

III

KETTERINGHAM

THE church of Ketteringham goes back to Domesday Book and beyond. It was a little church without aisles, once capable of seating perhaps 150 people, with wide, low, enclosed pews, a three-decker pulpit, a medieval font carved with roses and climbing grapes, and a decaying roof, set upon medieval corbels, not to be mistaken for the fine roof with its angels and shields and emblems and bosses which the visitor will now see and which dates from the year 1908. A hundred yards away to the south-east, stands Ketteringham Hall, the home of the squires; and the church is richly ornamented with their memorials, a little sanctuary enshrining the long history of the parish from the days of the Norman landlords. Roger Bigod had taken the land from its Saxon lord; the Argentines had lived here, and then the Greys, and then the Heveninghams — barons and crusaders and merchant-knights, leaving their monuments in brass or stone, scrolls and canopies and urns and lozenges. One of the Heveninghams had helped to try King Charles I and had been attainted as a regicide; but his widow, Lady Mary Heveningham, erected a monument for all her family and 'her deceased husband', though she would not mention his name. The church is a microcosm of the history of England.

The wall upon the south side of the churchyard was also the wall of the squire's garden. To walk northwards from the front door of the Hall was to pass the servants' quarters, and then the stables, and then the church. Standing almost beneath the shadow of the Hall, the church must have seemed in earlier days like a private chapel to the squire; and sometimes its vicar must have seemed in earlier days like the private chaplain of the squire. In 1831, there were only twenty-eight inhabited houses in the village, a few of them outlying farms, but mostly groups of cottages scattered down the lane beyond the church. The parish consisted of the Hall and the tenants of the squire;

and sometimes the vicar seemed only like a superior tenant. Sir Henry Grey, who built the chancel of the church in the later fifteenth century, was not silent upon the squire's rightful place in his church. For he (unless it were perhaps his heirs) placed a noble figure of himself in the central light of the great east window; and so his portrait in stained glass looked down upon the nave and dominated the simple worshippers. When Andrew came to Ketteringham, the east window had long been smashed, no one knows how, and little fragments of its loveliness had been replaced, higgledy-piggledy, and not in the seemly order wherein they may now be found.

In a measure, the glory had departed by 1835. The incumbent of the church since 1786 had been Dr. Miles Beevor, the offspring of a distinguished family in Norfolk. Dr. Beevor concerned himself with politics and with hunting. He possessed two other livings and resided upon one of them, and he came to Ketteringham only to perform his duty. If he found no congregation waiting, he locked the church and rode home, uncomplaining. The people ceased to bother to attend their church, the normal congregation was the clerk and three others, the cobwebs gathered, the fabric began to decay. Sometime between 1814 and 1835 a whole tomb standing in the chancel vanished, the tomb of that Sir Henry Grey whose portrait had looked out from the east window.

Perhaps if the squire had been resident, the non-residence of Dr. Beevor would have mattered less. But Ketteringham Hall, like Ketteringham church, seemed to have passed the days of its splendour. The Heveninghams had sold it in 1717 to a Mr. Edward Atkyns, and his family was still in possession when Andrew arrived—indeed it was through a connexion between Miss Atkyns and the Wickes family that Mrs. Wickes had secured the paper parcel containing the presentation to the living.

Once the Atkyns family might have maintained its state as proudly as any Grey or Heveningham. The Atkyns monument in the church bids fair to rival the monuments of its predecessors. It reminds the visitor of certain solid and prosaic qualities of the eighteenth century; perhaps a little wordy, perhaps a little unromantic, perhaps a little florid. We think no longer of crusaders or of regicides, but of worthy Englishmen with sound digestions and prudent minds, versed in polite literature. But if the family had once been opulent and reputed, it had lately been impoverished by one of the most romantic and colourful ladies of her time.

Mrs. Edward Atkyns had come into Norfolk from a career on the stage, and devoted her widowhood to rescuing the Queen of France or the Dauphin from the prisons of the French Revolution. Upon this fruitless task she gave away large sums of money, sometimes to dishonest men who promised what they had no intention of performing. She filled Ketteringham Hall with French émigrés and Bourbon conspirators; her endeavours for the Tory party in the county election of 1806 make one of the most amusing bypaths in the history of Norfolk.[1] She mortgaged the estate, and after the battle of Waterloo was forced to retire to France, where she vainly pursued her plea that she should be repaid the £80,000 which she claimed to have spent in the service of the Bourbon monarchs. When Andrew came to the parish of Ketteringham, Mrs. Atkyns was dying in Paris, poor and resentful, living in a squalor redeemed by her private world of fantasy, believing that she had almost succeeded in a heroic attempt to rescue Queen Marie Antoinette. Ketteringham Hall was leased to strangers. When Andrew arrived, it was rented by a Mr. Ogilby.

The Hall was still a noble mansion of Tudor times, with a wooded park of 500 acres, a small lake, and a stream running through it to join the river Yare. But its squire was not a ruler of his parish like Sir Henry Grey, or Lady Mary Heveningham. He was the tenant of a destitute old lady, a superior tenant, but still renting of the absentee as the gamekeeper rented his cottage, and renting land which everyone knew to be mortgaged to the limit.

The benefice of Ketteringham was poor. The people, inhabiting their twenty-eight houses, numbered (in 1831) 215 souls. With the exception of Mr. Ogilby, they were labourers, servants, gardeners, carpenters, rising to small tenant-farmers. The living carried with it thirty-eight acres of glebe land, and otherwise was almost entirely dependent upon tithes. Andrew's

[1] R. W. Ketton-Cremer, *A Norfolk Gallery*, pp. 215 ff. The chief Atkyns monument is at the end of the south transept of Westminster Abbey.

stipend amounted in aggregate to under £200. Perhaps in the old days of noble squires the vicar had received much benefit from the Hall. In the days of Mrs. Atkyns, Dr. Miles Beevor had relied upon his pluralities and his private means.

Andrew was the incumbent of no other parishes, but his private means, derived from the property in Northamptonshire, were substantial. He could afford to be independent of the hazards of tithe collection, independent even of a Mrs. Atkyns. And therefore he at once found himself, as none of his predecessors had found themselves, the most important person in the parish in the eyes of the parishioners. His predecessors had failed to reside, or, if they resided, had been dominated by the powerful squire or his lady. Andrew was vicar of Ketteringham alone, in rank he was the equal of the gentleman living on sufferance at the Hall, and his wife's family was friendly with Miss Atkyns, an authentic representative of the squirearchy of the Hall. It was unfortunate, in the light of what was about to happen to the Hall, that he began his parochial ministry in the rare situation of being able to master his squire.

Mr. Ogilby was not comfortable. Andrew had always believed in being direct from the pulpit, and his directions could sometimes touch personalities. The people were not a little afraid of him. He started by distributing daily texts for the children to learn. Passing down the street a few weeks after his arrival, he saw a lad stacking mangel-wurzel and stopped and looked over the hedge to watch him. The lad said guiltily, 'Please, sir, I've not got a paper!' Mr. Ogilby was likewise afraid. Andrew, who never moderated a denunciation of sin, thought that he and his household were iniquitous, and at least once intruded the opinion into a sermon. And then he thought that he observed Mr. and Mrs. Ogilby twice laughing during service.

He determined to call at the Hall and rebuke them. He went there on Sunday after service and, when the servants brought Mr. Ogilby to him, said, 'Mr. Ogilby, I doubt not you will be surprised at the purport of my visit. But the office of a minister is a very responsible one. I was sorry on Sunday last to see Mrs. Ogilby laugh at the time of service; and though I know you did not consider the sin of it, it hurt me much to see and I hope it may not be repeated.' The blood rushed to Ogilby's cheek, his tongue faltered, his whole frame became contorted (as it seemed to Andrew), and with great vehemence he said, 'I assure you, sir, I never laughed.'

'No,' said Andrew, 'I only saw Mrs. Ogilby.'

'I never intended any insult to you,' said Ogilby.

'I am quite satisfied, sir, of that,' said Andrew. 'If I had thought that, perhaps I could not have come with so great calmness, but *I* could have thought little of it. But I am sure as a minister of Christ you will see that I must and ought to be very jealous for God's honour. Besides, the effect upon the poor must be very injurious.' After a few softer words, Andrew held out his hand. The squire hesitated whether to take it and then protruded two fingers.

Andrew went home persuaded that he had been at fault. He had known that the duty was unpleasant and so had postponed it. By postponing it he had made it more unpleasant. He convinced himself (unfortunately, as it was to prove) that hard duties are harder in prospect than reality.

*   *   *   *   *

In 1836, a year after Andrew came, Mrs. Atkyns died, still dreaming in the garret at the Rue de Lille. She bequeathed Ketteringham Hall to a relative whose death had preceded hers by a few months. In her will she desired that her body be taken to Ketteringham and interred within the family vault beneath the chancel of the church, and that her name and age be inscribed upon a plain marble slab upon the walls. Her relatives, whose fortune she had dissipated by the pursuit of her fairy kingdom, felt these desires to be improper and failed to execute them. And thus it happened that Ketteringham Hall was offered for sale.

Within a few weeks came the news that the Hall had been bought by a Mr. John Peter Boileau. Soon Ogilby was leaving Ketteringham, and a rumour reached the parish that he had gone mad and died, crying, 'The devils are about me.' Andrew wrote the widow an affectionate letter which is extant.

For two years after the death of Mrs. Atkyns, no Boileau inhabited the Hall at Ketteringham. There was infinite speculation and gossip in the parish about him and his family. They heard, no doubt with gratification, that their new squire had been raised to the rank of baronet at the coronation of Queen Victoria. They heard that he possessed a beautiful and aristocratic wife, the Lady Catherine Sarah Elliott, third daughter of the Earl of Minto, formerly Governor-General of India. Andrew probably knew that Lady Catherine's father had raised a public storm by restraining the endeavours of missionaries in India. In the church services they remembered Boileau with an expectant hope, mingled in the minds of some with a measure of trepidation. Andrew knew well that the wrong kind of squire could ruin the souls of his parishioners. But he sometimes persuaded himself that anything for which he prayed fervently must come about, and was occasionally indignant when it failed. Over his new squire he prayed so fervently, and felt assured that all would be well.

The first authentic news came from the new bishop. In 1837 Dr. Bathurst had at last died, to the satisfaction of some among his clergy, at the age of ninety-three. The new bishop, Edward Stanley, was a different kind of man. He was a Whig in politics, appointed by a Whig prime minister, and therefore resembled his predecessor in not being *persona grata* to all the country clergy of the Norwich diocese. (There was Tacey, a neighbouring parson, who was asked by an eminent person — was it Dr. Stanley? — visiting his school, what he taught the children, and is said to have replied, 'To fear God, honour the Queen, and hate the Whigs.') But Stanley was a humane, liberal-minded, comparatively active man; and to feel a new effectiveness at the centre of ecclesiastical administration predisposed his clergy to perceive his excellence. The slack and the criminal disliked his arrival. Andrew, though not naturally disposed to admire dignities, at first took to him.

The bishop surprised his clergy by inviting them to the palace; and there they met some of the leading men of the county, lay or ecclesiastical. Andrew found his first visits to the palace to be delightful evenings. Bishop Stanley, it appeared, knew Sir John Boileau. 'He is one of the most religious and best of men I ever knew. I quite congratulate you, Mr. Andrew. I said, "Boileau, if you go into Norfolk, I shall have no objection to accepting the bishopric".' He offered Andrew a letter of introduction to Boileau; but Andrew, with his characteristically independent sense of what was fitting, thought that no introduction ought to be necessary between a minister and his squire. He committed a warning to his diary. 'I cannot but feel his Lordship's kindness to me is very marked. O may I be in my watch tower! How easily does pride insinuate itself.' From the pulpit he told his congregation what the bishop had said of Sir John.

By early October, 1838, the Hall was again inhabited. On Sunday morning a whole party from the Hall attended service and occupied the squire's pew—Lady Catherine, four children, a governess and four or five servants. Andrew was too unwell to take the service, and his duty was performed by a neurotic curate named Holmes. They seemed attentive, and told him that Sir John was kept in London by gout. A few days after, the squire himself came into residence. Andrew at once called on him.

The new squire put into words what was hidden in Andrew's mind. 'I know, Mr. Andrew, a squire is often considered a blessing but my opinion is they are a curse.' Andrew gave a silent assent. He thought the proposition undeniable. Squires brought with them a household of servants, strangers to the village, with their own ways and their own loyalties. The servants of a squire had the reputation of having the hardest husks for any incumbent to crack. Nor was he impressed by what he saw of the Boileau servants. He summed them up damningly as 'scarcely superior to poor Mr. Ogilby's.' However, he rejoiced at the new squire's declaration that he wished to go hand in hand with the vicar in seeking the welfare of his people, though he pinned no extravagant hopes upon the declaration. He began to think of Sir John as a 'lay-coadjutor'. To be a lay-coadjutor, however, was not to be Sir John's idea of his own function.

Andrew perceived that Boileau was a very different man from poor Mr. Ogilby. He remembered that he and his wife had adopted a principle of refusing all invitations to dinner, and he uneasily expected the inevitable invitation from the new squire. He even composed a little speech, prepared for the awkward occasion. It came quickly. On 14th November, Sir John Boileau took Andrew for a long ride, and invited him to dinner for the following day. Andrew launched into his prepared refusal.

'I feel, Sir John, I may speak frankly to you, and I doubt not you will understand me. We have had frequent invitations to dinner at Hudson Gurney's[1] and elsewhere; and finding visiting would intrude greatly upon our parochial duties, and, accepting one, refusing another would be very marked, we determined to continue the plan we adopted on our union of declining any formal invitation to dinner; but I feel and thank you for your kindness. We should be happy at any future time to join you in the evening at tea.'

'Well,' said the squire, 'I hope and think you will see it right to make a distinction between your Parishioner and others.'

Ellen and her husband later went to an evening tea. The vicar enjoyed it and hoped that it was profitable. He judged Sir John to be a very clever man, kind and free, very liberal in political sentiments, an advocate for national education 'in which I could not join him. But in this I assented, that if our church catechism was the only obstacle to the admission of the children of dissenters into our school, they should not be compelled to learn it.'

The bishop had been right. The new squire was not only a wealthy man, but a civilized man. He was turning himself into a truly learned antiquarian, and his taste was excellent. But he was a man with a will. Every squire worth his salt was the master of his parish, and he could not be the master of his parish unless he were also master of its vicar. The vicar had independent means, a stern Calvinistic character, and a habit of ruling the parish before the new squire even arrived. Sir John Boileau was doubtless aware of these difficulties. But he knew what was due to him and intended to get his way. It was therefore inevitable that Church and State in Ketteringham should clash. And it was fortunate indeed for the parish and the vicar that the newcomer was a man who would not be likely to suspect insult or injury, and who would not stand upon his dignity.

On 1st December, Sir John, perhaps determined to break down his vicar's resistance to accepting an invitation to dinner, requested Andrew to dine with him to meet the bishop and his family. Andrew's first instinct was to decline. But he felt, as Sir

[1] The antiquary and head of the great banking family of Gurneys, who lived at Keswick Hall.

John felt too, that he would be lacking in courtesy to his bishop if he declined. Ellen was ill and unable to go with him.

It did not please him that the conversation at the dinner-table was entirely on the subject of pedigree. When the cloth was removed, finger glasses were taken round so that the gentlemen might rinse their mouths. Andrew detested the idea, repudiated it as a worldly habit, refused to follow the example of the other men and thought it deplorable that the bishop should do so. When the ladies withdrew, Sir John gave a hint that he wished Ketteringham church was not so crowded with strangers but that people would keep to their own parish and leave room for the people of Ketteringham. Andrew replied, 'Many of my people will not regularly come and I cannot shut my doors against those that will even though from other parishes.' He turned to the bishop for his support. 'Throw open the doors and by no means hinder any,' the bishop said warmly, 'and if a person is not seated in their pew by the first lesson, fill it — unless it be locked up and then you can't force it.'

The subject of conversation was thereupon changed. But later, Sir John said, 'I think, Mr. Andrew, one sermon would be quite enough for us.' Andrew was glad to notice that the bishop looked his surprise. 'No sir,' said Andrew, 'I have been accustomed to five duties weekly and I can't reduce it to less than two.'[1] He went home perturbed, and what he wrote in his diary would have surprised the squire. 'The cloven foot here showed itself. I now fear Sir John is a designing man, he attends church only once daily (i.e. once a Sunday), talks much on secular matters on the Sabbath, all which things speak much. The evening was spent in relating ridiculous anecdotes of children, in short in a manner not becoming the gospel of Christ. I think I shall not go again!'

A month later, on 2nd January, squire and parson were in vehement argument whether you must moralize the people before you Christianize them or whether you must Christianize them in order to moralize. It was characteristic of Andrew that he should feel all not to be right between himself and the squire until he had summoned the courage to rebuke him for something. Sir John's idea of the squire's duty did not coincide with

[1] Dr. Lubbock had recently ordered Andrew not to give lectures, for his health's sake, and limited him to two sermons.

the vicar's idea of the squire's duty. The squire liked the good things of this life and enjoyed them as God's gifts. When he had visitors — and he often had visitors — he entertained them to a game of cards. Andrew was troubled beyond measure when he found that his people began to defend themselves, before his denunciation of similar levities, by appealing to the example of the squire. The *casus belli* arose when he heard from a dissenter that Sir John had accepted the office of steward at the Norwich races.

On 15th April, 1839, therefore, Andrew wrote to Sir John a frank letter upon his whole conduct as a professing Christian. A copy of the letter has survived. Andrew described the hopes and prayers which he and his people had directed on behalf of their new squire; and he asked that if Sir John saw anything amiss in his own conduct as an ambassador of Christ he should administer reproof. 'But greatly as I desire that we should co-operate in the welfare of the flock I cannot see it practicable unless we first decide upon adopting the same principles. . . . You cannot uphold my ministerial character if you deny the truth of my pulpit statements . . . What must the people think if on the authority of God's word I condemn the pleasures of the world and they hear that you advocate balls and plays? If I teach them to reverence God's Sabbath and not to "forsake the assembling of themselves together", and they perceive that you slight his ordinance and do your own pleasure on that day? You might perhaps suppose that poor simple cottagers would not notice these things. But I assure you, their continual remarks on these subjects have been the source of the sorrow of which I complain. Whenever I have advanced anything for the support of your influence, they have stopped me, by reminding me of such things as in their estimation seemed incompatible with vital Christianity. But that which has brought my grief to a crisis and urged me as a minister of the Gospel thus to address you is a late report that you have become steward of the Norwich races.'

Sir John answered the letter with courtesy; but Andrew felt trepidation as to what he would say when they next met. At that meeting the squire did not mention the letter; he mentioned only that he would be leaving the country for a considerable time. But the vicar heard with a leap of pleasure that he had resigned the office of steward at the Norwich races. It was again unfortunate, in the light of the future, that Andrew attributed the resignation to his own letter, whereas truth would seek the squire's motive in the plans for his journey abroad. Andrew was gaining a misleading idea, almost a fantasy, of what his words could effect with Sir John Boileau.

Sir John, so soon after his arrival at Ketteringham, was going abroad because the doctors feared for his wife unless he took her to a warmer climate. Lady Catherine was suffering from that undiagnosed malady which hampered her and her husband for the rest of her life — part nerves perhaps, part bronchial, part digestive. On 17th July, 1839, Boileau left London for Dover, with his wife and children, a tutor (Mr. Bickmore), a governess, and four servants, all travelling in three carriages. He took them to Geneva, Nice, and Northern Italy. After only a few months in the parish, therefore, the new squire left it to its own devices for two years. The conflict between Hall and vicarage was postponed.

*   *   *   *   *

Sir John was abroad until the summer of 1841, and while he was away, two events in Ketteringham affected our history, both through orders which he had given.

In 1840, he was observed to be building a hall. The modern visitor at once applies to this hall the epithet Gothick, so spelt. And a Gothick hall was what Sir John intended to build. It was designed to be a noble imitation of a medieval hall in which he would give balls and other splendid entertainments for the county, a hall fit for hospitalities rivalling the banquets of old England, and to be used by the servants as a dining-hall at times when there were no hospitalities. Its ceiling was covered, at a cost of £20, with oil paintings of the Boileau arms, the pelican in her piety above the family shield and the motto *De tout mon cœur.*

In Sir John's absence abroad, the hall rose from the ground. There was much guessing in the village as to what purpose the hall would serve. It was rumoured, on the architectural evidence, that Sir John had turned Catholic upon the continent and was building a chapel for the priest whom he was bringing home. Then it was rumoured, on better evidence, that the new hall was likely to be used for dancing. Andrew disapproved privately and publicly of dancing. He heard the rumour with grief. On 18th May, 1840, he happened to be passing the hall and walked near the workmen engaged upon it. One of them, hoping for a conventional tip, accosted him:

'Sir, will you please to lay a brick?'

'O yes,' said Andrew, 'if you will tell me how I can.'

'I'll show you, sir.'

'Tell me, my good fellow,' said Andrew, 'how this can be done? I preach to my people against dancing. What will they say if I were to help to build a dancing room?'

The workman said nothing. Another labourer had heard the exchange and approached, believing himself to possess an argument from the Bible. 'Did not Christ turn water into wine that they might have plenty to drink, and besides, sir, should you not do a poor fellow good when you can?'

Andrew said, 'Go and ask my poor people my opinion of that.' After further talk, the workman said, 'Well, sir, those men on the other side are building only a garden wall. If you give to them, it will be just the same.'

'That's a different matter,' said Andrew. 'I'll see about that, my good fellow.' He resolved to walk back that way in a day or two with a present for them so that they might not think his religious scruples caused a meanness in tipping.

On 22nd October, Andrew happened to be walking by with his close friend Philpot, archdeacon of the Isle of Man till 1838 and always addressed as Archdeacon thereafter.[1] They observed at one end the preparations for an orchestra. 'Come,' said Archdeacon Philpot with distaste and in the hearing of the workmen, 'we have had enough of this. Let us go and see the house of God.'

*   *   *   *   *

Ketteringham possessed no parsonage house. There was not a building in the parish but the Hall and the cottages. In those days when many incumbents failed to reside, and many parishes were shepherded by curates in lodging, this was not surprising. When Andrew first came to the parish, he rented Hethel Hall

[1] There is a charming life of Philpot by A. G. Bradley, entitled *Our Centenarian Grandfather*.

upon a short lease. A house less imposing than its name suggested, it had the merit of being only a mile from Ketteringham church. It had the demerit of being outside the parish and in the parish of Hethel.

He held Hethel Hall upon an insecure tenure. It had been the residence of one branch of the Beevor family, until an eccentric baronet, wearing knee-breeches and a costume of his own invention, preferred to live at Great Yarmouth. In 1840, while the Boileaus were touring the continent, Andrew heard that Hethel Hall and its estate were being put up for sale by its owner. He contemplated buying it if he could succeed in buying a part of the estate; but in September, 1840, he heard that Sir John had bought Hethel Hall. On 6th April, 1841, he received notice from Sir John's agent that he must quit Hethel Hall by Michaelmas of that year.

Boileau, absent abroad, had left the matter to his agent. Even when in England, he was far too busy to manage his own estate. He appointed a manager, trusted him sometimes beyond what was wise, intervened occasionally and heavily with decision or criticism; but until he heard of disaster, he was in the habit of leaving his managers to decide all matters of detail. From a distance, he approved the purchase of Hethel Hall; and it never seems to have occurred to him, until too late, that he was thereby ejecting his vicar from the only available vicarage. When he was able to give his personal attention to the problem, Hethel Hall was already his, his agent had served a notice upon the vicar three months before, and he had already promised the house to another. It was rumoured in Ketteringham that Sir John intended Hethel Hall as a dower-house. During the continental tour his boys' tutor Mr. Bickmore had engaged the affections of Miss Parmand, the children's governess. They were married in Ketteringham church on 14th July, 1841, and moved into Hethel Hall when the Andrews moved out. There they founded a preparatory school, to which aristocratic friends of the Boileaus were encouraged to send their boys.

Sir John never seems to have been aware that he was treating his vicar inconsiderately. And perhaps he was not displeased that Andrew needed to move house. If it vexed him that Christian men and women should not be attending their parish churches, it vexed him also that his own clergyman should be living outside his own parish. Perhaps Sir John would not have repined too deeply — for in 1841 he had known the parish for only six months — if his strategy about houses persuaded or compelled Andrew to resign Ketteringham. The squire could not see his parish running to his satisfaction until he had appointed his own clergyman with the advowson which he had purchased together with the estate. But Sir John was a man of honour. He would not, precisely, have wished to force Andrew out of the parish; or at least, if he persuaded Andrew to resign the benefice, he would have used his influence with the potent in Church and State to secure him a better benefice. Though he would not yet have admitted to himself that he wished to drive Andrew out of the parish, he would perhaps have admitted that he would have liked to drive Andrew *into* the parish; and that if he failed in this endeavour, he would not have been sorry to see Andrew resign.

To Andrew it looked as though he must resign. He had secured a written permission from Dr. Stanley to reside anywhere within three miles of Ketteringham church. He surveyed the countryside within that radius and saw nothing that was even possible. There were five or six houses of the gentry, and a few large cottages. In those days it was unthinkable that an incumbent and a gentleman should not live in the house of a gentleman. Cringleford Hall had just been sold; Stanfield Hall had a resident; Mangreen Hall, a gaunt, solitary house, was three and a half miles; Miss Berney might be travelling and therefore ready to let Bracon Hall for a few months. A house at Wreningham, let with a farm, seemed possible. Was it within three miles? On 13th April, 1841, Andrew borrowed Mrs. Watt's wheel and measured the shortest route from Wreningham to Ketteringham church, ejaculating as he walked along with the wheel, 'Lord, hinder me if not for Thy glory.' He found it three miles and a little more, and could think of no route to save the distance. Mr. Ewing had a house at Cringleford — surely it was within the distance? The wheel reckoned it three miles and a furlong. Perhaps a furlong could be saved if all the corners were cut? But when he called at the house he found that Mr. Ewing's tenant had no desire whatever to leave.

The time was running short, and still he could not decide

what to do. He must find another living and quickly — Saxlingham perhaps. The bishop, he thought, might allow him to take another living with a good parsonage, live in the parsonage, and pay a curate for Ketteringham. 'That would increase my non-residents,' said the bishop, who was steadily reducing the percentage of non-residents in his diocese. The bishop thought that Sir John might help him to build a parsonage; Andrew thought that Sir John would be unlikely to do anything so calculated to keep his present incumbent in office. His advisers were not always agreed. The penniless Sharpe said, 'Go and buy the first thing you can at any price.' Philpot recommended him to wait as long as possible and thus give the bishop and Sir John a chance to find him another benefice. 'I know not what will be,' wrote Andrew, 'but by God's grace I purpose to lie meekly in the hands of Sir John and the bishop.' It was a promise which he found impossible to keep.

In July, 1841, with less than three months to run, the bishop withdrew the limit of three miles and said that he was ready to licence the nearest available house. The possibilities were now wider — he might rent Mr. Papillon's house in Wymondham (three and a half miles); he might live in Norwich if the worst befell. A few days later he heard that Mr. Burton was selling his house in Hethersett. It was too small, and if Andrew took it, he would have to build. Mr. Burton, moreover, was believed to be asking an exorbitant price. But it was near to Ketteringham.

Andrew owned property in Northamptonshire and was well-endowed with this world's goods, but it was his strict religious principle not to be extravagant. During the next fortnight or more he was engaged in a vehement struggle with his conscience, whether he would be right to pay an exorbitant price for the only possible house within a reasonable distance of Ketteringham.

Burton demanded the sum of £4,000; and in consequence Andrew ordered his agent to rent Mr. Papillon's house in Wymondham. He spent a miserable Sunday (18th July) able to think of nothing but the house, too conscious of the text, 'Be anxious for nothing.' Part of his trial was his wife and his wife's mother, who continued to agitate that he should buy the house at Hethersett. On 15th August, with six weeks to run, he attended the auction in Norwich. He had two agents in the room, ready to bid up to £3,500. In the event he pushed the price to £3525, only to be told the reserve price was £4000 and the house was withdrawn. He was now as uncertain what to do as ever before. Two days later, Butcher, the auctioneer, came to his house and offered him the Hethersett house for £3,700. Andrew, though he was now determined to have the house ('Hethersett surely is the place marked out for us by God! This morning I had a season of sweet communion with the Lord and was enabled to plead with him strongly about Hethersett'), refused to go beyond £3,600. On 18th August the offer was accepted, and he was to live at Wood Hall, Hethersett, for more than forty years. It is a most charming house of old brick, entered by a narrow archway with a parvise above, protected from the main road by a belt of great trees.

Sir John was not pleased. His vicar had left Hethel, which was outside the parish, and found himself a house at Hethersett, which was also outside the parish and as far from Ketteringham church. Andrew, on his side, was persuaded that Sir John, perhaps with the complaisance of the bishop, had tried to drive him from Ketteringham.

* * * * *

To understand this history, it is necessary to be familiar with the unusual character of Andrew, his forcible religion, and his place among the parishioners. To that end I insert a few extracts from his diary, written during the period while Sir John was touring upon the continent and soon after he had returned.

1839

July — I have ever been rather a congregational than a parochial minister. My present congregation is every Sabbath made up from at least six or seven parishes. Lord, I feel the privilege. May I esteem it more and more and use it more for thy glory.

16 September — Day of wonders! and almost the day of judgment! O may I never forget it! this is the third time the Lord has manifestly redeemed my life from the grave. Having had an interesting voyage from Norwich to Yarmouth, nursing some young ladies ill of the hooping-cough and making a general distribution of tracts with some success among the rich as well as poor, I determined to

proceed with our new intended housemaid A. Cannell (my child in the Gospel) towards Gorleston on foot; but whilst carrying my bag across to Mr. Teasdel's, a lad cried 'Are you going to London, sir?' I answered in the negative and added I was going to Gorleston. He replied, 'They will take you there, sir.' I spoke to the Captain, who said, 'I must stop, sir, at the pier to take on board a cargo of herrings.' This was delightful. Without hesitation I with my female servant was quickly on deck. In a few minutes we were moving, and soon came in contact with another vessel, but no injury. Approaching the pier I waved my hand to Ellen at the window but did not think she saw me. *Ramona* (the steamer on which we were aboard) came near the side of the pier but was carried back by the stream nearly to the destruction of a fine brig lying in the harbour. Ropes were then cast out to lash her to the pier but they were quickly broken, and I had the agony of hearing the Captain give the word for going to sea. As we passed the pier head, I entreated the Captain to put me in a boat. I cried out in agony to the pilots, several of whom I knew by name but the Captain only answered with a look of dismay and vociferous oaths and the pilots did not attempt to stir about. We were now at sea; never shall I forget the billows at the mouth of the harbour. On crossing the bar, twice we struck aground. The Captain now told me he dared not attempt to stop till he got to London, and that two of his Yarmouth agents were in the same predicament as myself. I again urged the necessity, if possible, of my getting to land. He said he would do his utmost, but there was no hope. He however would hoist the baif, i.e. the flag of distress, for a boat, but as we passed Corton the boats remained quiet on the shore. I now seated myself calmly by the side of my female companion. The sea now became alarming and roared terribly, the proud waves lifted up themselves, every fresh billow seemed as though it would dash in pieces the fore part of the vessel. The wind increased and the passengers were aptly described by the Psalmist, 'They reel to and fro like drunken men and are at their wits end.' The Captain at the bows and the steerer at the helm anxiously watched each other; but one gentleman to whom I mentioned my anxiety about my dear Ellen sympathised with me. It was not merely the danger I was in occupied my thoughts. I could know nothing about my dear wife. Did she know that I was on board the vessel or would she fear that I was ill at Hethel? Would she be alarmed at my voyage during the approaching night, for it was now about three o'clock and we should not reach town till about noon on the morrow. All was uncertain! I knew nothing! Besides all this she was soon expecting her confinement. With these thoughts I said 'Well, Anne, this is sad but we are in the hands of God!' She sweetly and calmly replied, 'O yes, sir, He will take care of us.' I now committed my soul to my Saviour's care, praised Him that I was enabled to be so calm and resigned in this trying season. I also examined my future hopes. I felt comfort having again and again left myself in the hands of God. I began to consider how I could make myself useful among the passengers and arranged that if we should be sinking during the voyage, I might imitate the conduct of holy Foster and call upon the agonising company to seek mercy through a Redeemer. I was about to distribute my tracts when my sympathising friend exclaimed, 'There's a boat off!' I started from my seat, but the vessel pitched in such a manner that I was nearly lying upon my face. I looked for my companion, her head hung over the side of the vessel, her face was ghastly pale. I told her the tidings and scarcely had I collected my luggage than the boat was in sight — but now it struck me, 'Will it not be at the hazard of our lives that we get into the boat?' I asked the Captain. He replied, 'I think you'll live at sea. It will be the worst when you come to land.' What could be done? The men had come, putting their lives into their hands. The Captain would rage if we refused but above all there was a hope of seeing my darling wife that evening. Anne with firm step and sweet calmness cast herself into the arms of the intrepid boatmen. I threw my bag to the bottom of the boat and placed myself upon it, lest a wave might wash me overboard. The steamer's paddles were again in motion, but our danger now was more imminent. The boatmen insisted upon being towed for some distance by the steamer. Our little boat was all but under the paddles. I begged of them to let go the rope. How suitable were the words of David at this moment, Psalm lxix. 14, 15. I do indeed say, If the Lord had not now been on our side the waters had over-whelmed us, the stream had gone over our soul, the proud waters had gone over our soul, Ps. cxxiv. After gradually slackening the rope we were left alone to combat with the waves. I still felt happy — but how shall I declare it! On turning to look at my partner in distress I perceived the arm of the pilot round her waist and he evidently intoxicated uttering improper sentences. The two rowers were little better and the two agents indulging in profane jests. Thus innumerable evils encompassed us about but we were now close to shore when a heavy billow threatened to swallow us up quick but it broke under us and the succeeding one drove us on to the beach one over the other. My leg was severely bruised, and when I recovered and looked around I found they had brought Anne safe to shore. My feelings of gratitude at this time must be felt to be understood. I trust it may not be like the morning dew but rather like David's sin, 'ever before me'. One of the boatmen according to my direction followed me with our baggage to Mr. Cunningham's at Lowestoft, at which place we were put on shore. He was from home. I was preparing a note to ask him to give shelter to my servant till six o'clock when the van would convey her to Gorleston. At this moment he came in and after my narration and his recovery from his astonishment that any boat should venture to sea on such a day, he laughed heartily and pressed me to wait and dine with him very soon. I did so. During dinner I enquired about a coach. He said there was one to Yarmouth through Gorleston almost directly. Scarcely had he spoke when something like a van or waggon passed the window, and he exclaimed, 'There is your coach.' I hastened and found nothing more or less than a carrier's cart. I thought of dear Ellen and gladly took a seat in anything that would convey me to her. We placed ourselves at the back part of the cart. In a few minutes the two agents now intoxicated placed themselves in front of us, and scarcely had we gone two miles when two women with two children begged to be taken up as they had been insulted by a very suspicious looking man. I now found a sufficient assembly to begin preaching. We were thirteen in number. The women were affected to tears. I distributed tracts and on reaching Gorleston as a trifling thankoffering for my mercy I paid the fare of the poor women and running my umbrella through my carpet bag Anne and I trudged along in the dark to Mr. King's. I feared to knock. I dare not speak. I knew not how to enter. At last I opened the door and coughed; and in an instant was in Ellen's arms, when she gave the following account of herself. 'When the *Ramona* steamer passed, I had not a thought of you being in her but I observed there was something wrong when she went out of the harbour. Soon after Mr. Upjohn called to tell me not to be alarmed but you were on board and gone to London not being able to land; and then as a Job's comforter told me a tale of some friends of his who intending to land at a certain place in England were by mistake taken on to Madeira. Soon after this Captain Smith sent to say he thought he saw a boat put off from Lowestoft. I now started along the Lowestoft road when nearly dark, making enquiry of all I met till a gentleman told me, he had been at Lowestoft the whole day and it was utterly impossible that a boat could be got off from that place with such a sea; indeed some friends had desired to be put on board but it was not practicable. I now returned disconsolate, had a good cry, committed you to God, and felt more calm, expecting to see you when the vessel returned on Wednesday evening.' Lord, I know by thy word as also by past experience what a treacherous heart mine is. O in mercy keep it in a lively sense of this mercy, and grant that I may so pass through the waves of this troublesome world that I may come to the harbour of Eternal rest!

1840

4 December — The effect of my new medicine is astonishing! Thirling two years ago was at the brink of the grave and has had another attack of liver complaint. I began with brandy and salt, which at first produced a kind of intoxicated feeling, with increased headache and a warm glow through the whole frame. She persisted according to my prescribed plan, first rubbing the crown with about a tablespoonful and then the first thing in the morning taking internally the same quantity with double quantity of boiling water. She is much better. The cold fits are less, headache much relieved and pain between the shoulders almost gone and sickness quite cured. I could not but notice the improvement in her pulse from about 60 to 80. She is very grateful. May it be an open door for me to her soul. Lord, leave not her soul unhealed!

15 December — A day of trial and day of interest, may it prove a day of warning and profit. I received an invitation to a clerical meeting at Heigham and wrote an answer to say I would accept it for this day. On arriving, in a few minutes I asked what was his hour of meeting. He replied with an earnest look, "Tis not today.' Feeling ashamed at my carelessness I pretended to think it was not and said, 'No! next Tuesday.' Though I had come with only a slight doubt that this was the day. I tried to get out of my difficulty, but an attempt to extricate yourself from an evident deviation from honesty commonly plunges you the deeper. Thus it was with me. Seeing my note on the table I looked and saw that I had written to say I should come as today. I was obliged then to confess that I thought perhaps the meeting might be today. Having rested about half an hour, I started through the deep snow, my feet muffled with snowboots; for as I had not anticipated a return till the evening, it was useless waiting for the gig which I had ordered to meet me. Being nearly eight miles from home I urged my way through the falling snow; weeping, not at the idea of a weary walk, but that shame had prevented me from at once saying I had made a mistake in the day. For surely my deception is discovered. I do henceforth determine by God's grace to speak in simplicity and godly sincerity. Proceeding with a heavy heart I met with a circumstance which seemed to put fresh strength into my weary frame. When about half way home I saw a man felling a tree in a field. I called and said 'What are you felling that beautiful tree for?' Looking up, he said, "Tis, sir, a pretty tree but I

want to make this piece a garden and it brouses over so.' I replied, 'Yes, my good fellow, 'tis like some great man whose conduct is injurious to those under his influence and God in mercy cuts him down.' The man looked at me earnestly but said little. I then spoke to him about his soul and called him to receive some tracts. Approaching, he said, 'You preach at Ketteringham, sir, I used to come and hear you but I am so far off now.' The tears rolled rapidly down his cheeks whilst I spoke to him, and on leaving and taking him by the hand he wept much and said, 'O would you, sir, come and see me when you pass this way. I live in the cottage by the road side.' Who can tell but that my mistake about Heigham was to bring me in contact with this poor man! Proceeding on my journey, I visited the cottages at Intwood and heard of poor Mr. Drake whom I have seen from the pulpit spit frequently into the reading desk whilst preaching, and the other Sunday being completely lost in reading the service, the clerk raising his hand said, 'Sir, you are wrong.' When in great anger he exclaimed 'Then you ought to put me right.' When will such teachers be removed or converted! When, Lord, wilt Thou arise and have mercy on our Zion!

21 December — Deeply sympathising with the inhabitants of Silfield, I sallied forth in the snow on Saturday and having obtained from a farmer the names of the more distressed, I have this day been supplying their wants. I tried to go as a stranger but there was scarcely a cottage in which I was not recognised. I gave to each about five shillings in clothing. O what a privilege to be the Lord's Almoner! Remember me, O God, for good! Enlarge my heart! Let not my left hand know what my right has done!

1841

23 January — Having proclaimed that I would give soup to any persons on the Lizard who would think it worth while to walk seven or eight miles in deep snow, I found today thirty-three persons assembled at the door, to whom I gave from six to eight pints each, and I purpose (D.V.) to boil forty pounds of beef into soup weekly during the winter which together with about a peck of peas, a bundle of leeks and three or four papers of groats, boiled for ten hours, will afford nourishing food for upwards of forty families. One woman brought two boilers. I inquired the name of her neighbour she came for. She replied there was fifteen on the ticket and she thought it meant fifteen pints. I told her it was the day of the month on which she was to come. Poor things, they must be needy to walk so far for soup!

6 May — Confirmation at Wymondham. I had twelve, to four of whom I gave tickets of examined and approved, to the rest only examined and as mine were the only candidates with paper tickets instead of cards I thought that they would be the more noticed but I had determined boldly to say, 'I dare not give them my approval as being fit for confirmation, though I consider them not immoral.' How strange ministers urge thoughtless persons to attend. I cannot see how any impenitent worldling can present themselves, but I pressed upon my young people only two questions — what confirmation is, and what the things which their godfathers and godmothers did promise for them in baptism — but when the Bishop in his address exclaimed, looking at the clergy, 'Remember if there be any of these young persons who are not under religious impression, the fault is not theirs but yours, because you have failed in your duty,' I felt an earnest desire to contradict it, for it was like saying, 'It was of the will of man and not of God.' O how much did the Bishop say in his address to wound everyone acquainted with the Gospel of Christ, but I find the desire to speak of it quite a snare. Set a watch, O Lord, before my mouth and keep it.

9 May — Met the Bishop at breakfast at Tasburgh. Strange man! Behaved as though I had been a stranger. Expects you to advance your hand which I never will do; as Mrs. Weyland says, he is versed in every ology but The-ology. I should like to write to him on the subject of his address at Wymondham. Had it been in my church, I think I must have done so. It was Heterodoxy! At Tasburgh at the beginning of breakfast the Bishop at once sat down and Preston muttered something by way of grace. At the conclusion nothing was said. Lord grant that by the omissions of others I may learn wisdom.

1842

5 January — Drew tooth for old Mrs. Roberts. It was singular that I went to Ketteringham for the purpose of extracting it and I found her in great pain, upon which I drew from my pocket a pair of pincers which caused the poor old woman to shake and she begged I would use a piece of thread, I at last broke it off which perhaps was better than extracting the fangs.

26 February — Accepted office of rural dean . . . Miss Nash saw me felling a tree. I felt it might lower me in her sight as a minister. I do not feel satisfied about such employ for a minister. I do it for exercise and 'tis a delight, but if Paul would not eat meat if it made a brother to offend should I if it give offence, not that I ever heard

that it did, perhaps on the other hand it may show that a man of God can enjoy temporal recreations if consistent with other duties.

5 March — Joyful note from Miss Hardyman declaring the conversion of her sister who has for several Sundays been attending Ketteringham church. What hath God wrought! May this news excite me to greater diligence. The Lord cause her to grow till she come to the fulness of the measure of the stature of Christ. Feel more prepared for tomorrow than I have done for months. I determine by God's help I will digest my sermons better. I get more matter than I can digest and leave no time for putting it together. I have felt the great advantage of great abstinence today.

6 March — Famous congregations. Scapegoat an interesting subject also John xvii. 9. Children ruined for singing by Miss Boileau's training.

17 March — Preston called. Walked to Ketteringham church. He saw the family of *his* squire behaving indecorously in the house of God and called on Mr. G. to remonstrate, when Mr. G. took offence and left the church for six months, but his second daughter returned from a ball and soon died. Preston catching the favourable season used it to conciliate and effected his purpose. How faithful we should be in reproving and not look so much at consequences.

27 March — When leaving the vestry Mr. Bickmore wished to speak with me and soon producing a paper asked me to sign a petition against the income tax, at the same time apologising for the day. Of course I refused. Poor man could have little profited by my sermon.

29 March — Wood Rising clerical meeting. Twelve in number, the subject very interesting. The best means of promoting spirituality in the minds of ministers. I was listened to with attention till I mentioned temperance in eating as a means. Poor Peter Jeckel began to laugh and his jesting long continued. How quickly I see the failings of others; how careless of my own. My propositions were rejected for improving our meetings. I must have one of my own at Hethersett. I want more spiritual meetings.

1843

15 June — Elizabeth the cook, a valuable servant, insists on wearing a collar! What must dear Ellen do? The rule of the house is that such things should not be done. She says she will wear it or

leave. I say the law must not be broken and we must trust the Lord. After a few days I will speak to her but 'tis useless till her mind is calmed.

6 July — Mr. and Mrs. Preston spent the afternoon with us. I wish this friend was nearer. He says Sir John spoke of me in high terms but complains that I will not go out to dine.

12 July — Hay making day! Too much recreation . . . gave porter to six poor men and broth to three, they need strengthening at such a season. I have had too much exertion.

16 July — Preached from Joshua ii and Jeremiah ii 37 latter part. Good congregations. Boileaus returned, very courteous. But before Mrs. Andrew reached the church they had ordered the first and second classes of girls into their pew, when my dear Ellen properly countermanded the order saying she was the manager of the Sabbath School. How much they strive for mastery, but not lawfully. They aim at supremacy.

IV

SIR JOHN BOILEAU

SIR JOHN was descended from Charles Boileau, Baron de Castelnau and St. Croix, a Huguenot who had fled to England in 1691 from the persecutions of King Louis XIV. Behind the Huguenot stretched a long line of French aristocrats, a distinguished family of medieval lords and crusaders. One of them, Etienne Boileau, had been the Provost of Paris in 1260, and had governed Paris while Saint Louis IX prepared to sail upon his last crusade.

The Huguenot's son, Simeon, had become a merchant in Dublin. His son, John Peter, the father of our Sir John Peter, went out to India, became a member of the Council at Mazulipatam, and in 1785 returned from Madras to England with a fortune. Like many of the nabobs, he looked for a country estate, and so came into Norfolk by buying Tacolneston Hall, a few miles south of Ketteringham. He was still alive when his son bought Ketteringham Hall, and died in 1837, an old man aged ninety-one.

His son, John Peter of Ketteringham, was sent to Merton College in the University of Oxford. He pursued his studies further, sitting at the feet of the philosophers and scientists in Edinburgh — Hope, Playfair, Dugald Stewart. In the later stages of the wars against Napoleon, he entered the Rifle Brigade and served in the Netherlands under Lord Lynedoch. He took part in the capture of Bergen-op-Zoom and the assault upon Antwerp, and it was long afterwards a matter of pride to him that he had served as a brother officer with men like Havelock and Campbell. When Napoleon returned from Elba he was on leave in England. Though he posted day and night to join his regiment, he arrived twenty-four hours too late to fight in the battle of Waterloo. He bivouacked upon the boulevards when Wellington's troops occupied Paris. When peace came he studied law for a time under Sir J. T. Coleridge; but in 1825 he married the daughter of the Earl of Minto and settled down to the life of a country gentleman at Thursford Hall near Fakenham. As a local magistrate he helped to quell the riots of 1830 and received the thanks of the government.[1]

The returned nabobs who bought land in the country were frequently, and often justly, accused of pushing, of ostentation, of using their Indian wealth to batter at the gates of good breeding and landed tradition. Sir John Boileau was the son of a nabob; and his habits of building, his pride in his ancestry, his love of armorial insignia, his new Gothick hall, gave unpleasant neighbours a handle for their gossip. He once received an anonymous letter from a poison pen near Ketteringham which accused him of *novus homo* feelings. But he was much more secure and balanced than his occasional critics supposed. He at once took his rightful place among the leaders of the landed gentry in Norfolk, and without any sense of triumph, without any trace of aggression. He enjoyed high company, and was sorry when dukes and earls paid him little attention. But he was saved from any abnormal desire to climb, partly because he was of the second generation of Indian wealth, but mainly because he was a Boileau. He had no need to push his way into the circle of the great, because he assumed without thinking about it that this was the proper place for a descendant of crusading knights. He was no newcomer, thrusting himself upwards; on the contrary, most of the noble families of Norfolk had pushed their way upwards centuries after the Boileaus had been great.

His pride in the Boileau ancestry, though unaggressive, was nevertheless marked. Early in his time at Ketteringham, without consulting or telling the vicar, he erected upon the wall of the chancel a monument to his father, with an inscription which gives an account of the long antiquity of the family. After a few years, conscious that he inherited a historic tradition of squires, he found an eminent antiquary, Mr. Joseph Hunter; and with a generous subscription of £20 or so and some influence with the Norfolk and Norwich Archaeological Society, of which he was by then President, he caused Mr. Hunter to write and

---

[1] Authorities for his career: the monument which he erected to his father in Ketteringham church; Hunter in *Norfolk Archaeology*, vol. iii (1852), pp. 297-300; Connop Thirlwall, Presidential Address to the Royal Society of Literature, 21st April, 1869.

publish an admirable little essay, entitled *The History and Topography of Ketteringham*. He used to refer to it as 'my History', kept fifty copies to distribute, and preserved the engravings (the proofs of which are still to be found in the vestry at Ketteringham). The same poison pen accused him, unjustly, of paying for the whole volume, and imputed the motive that he wanted to tell everyone of his descent from the Barons of Castelnau. And yet the motive was not vulgar display, not even subtle display. He had a genuine archaeologist's interest in his own village and church and parish, and he wanted to encourage a model of local history. He was not displeased when Mr. Hunter inserted his ancestry; it seemed to him a matter for legitimate and proper pride. He examined his conscience when the poisonous letter arrived, and could not think that vanity or display had been his motives in being patron to Mr. Hunter.

The same charge has been laid against his Gothick hall. Unlike Mrs. Atkyns, Sir John Boileau had the means and the inclination to make this house a scene of splendid entertainments. It pleased him to be accepted upon equal terms by the lords of the land, and he had a keen sense of the due and decorous position which he wished to adorn. The Gothick richness of his hall illuminated one side of his character. It would be an exaggerated view to suppose that after reading the novels of Sir Walter Scott he imagined himself to be one of Scott's imaginary barons. But the hall was not intended to be ostentatious. The great east window is strong and elevating, but the body of the hall, with its panelling and at the west end its gallery and its pelicans upon a painted ceiling, must have been dark in daylight, even gloomy. The large old-fashioned fireplace, though striking, misses just too plainly the quality of magnificence. He was no spendthrift; the social climber would have spent his money freely to create the grandeur of his hall, and Sir John counted every pound. But partly because his ancestry was crusading, and partly because he lived in the new romantic age, he had a feeling which linked him to Norman knights. The visitor to Ketteringham, however, should be warned against blaming (or praising) Sir John for the massive evidence of Boileaus which is everywhere to be seen — pelicans in their piety prominent upon the gateposts of the churchyard, upon the village well, upon the white stanchions at the lodges;

in places expected and unexpected, they are to be found feeding the young with the blood from their breasts. Most of these armorial tokens date from many years after his death.

He was a man of medium height, of a darkish colouring, wavy dark brown hair, slightly severe features, a strong chin, brown eyes. He wore side whiskers and high collars, dressed with care, almost with precision; and gave people who met him the first impression of an old-fashioned and civilized courtesy, 'silvery' as someone said, which reminded them of his French ancestry. He had the keenest sense of the proprieties, and was painfully sensitive of any breach of them by himself or by anyone else. He was meticulous in the management of his affairs, was a frequent visitor to his lawyers, made a will of exceptional length, kept accounts even down to the tips when travelling, interviewed and employed and scolded and dismissed the male servants, butler and footmen and coachmen, in his household. At home his demands for orderliness, good manners, and discipline were severe. He regarded his servants as part of the family, as much a part of the family as his children, and felt their misbehaviours as breaches in the loyalty of the family more than as breaches of contract. Despite this careful side of his character, and the consequent economy of his expenditure, he was not a good manager of his own property. He was inclined to trust his own agents even beyond what was prudent, or allow them to go unsupervised for too long, and then be distressed when he found that their muddled accounts were incapable of sustaining his rigorous investigations of detail. Perhaps he suffered as a landowner from a faint sense of distaste, even a faint feeling that it would not be gentlemanlike to be too effective a manager of property. Experiments in agriculture, improvements of land, better drainage and more informed rotation of crops, in all these he was keenly interested. Just as he experimented in the house with a primitive machine for central heating called a calorifier, so he experimented in farming and made a just reputation as a benevolent and progressive landowner. But the return on his capital was negligible, and epidemically this worried him as he thought of his nine children.

The chief reason why he spent too little time over the management of his property in Norfolk or of his stocks and shares was simply that he had other and better affairs to attend, the affairs proper to a man of leisure. These affairs were not political. Though he was a prominent member of the Whig party, though his connexion with Lord John Russell through his marriage ensured him a direct access to the centre of the party, and though he sometimes held strong views on the subjects of the day, he would never have made a politician. He had too many scruples, too much uncertainty inside him, too much shrinking from clamour and hustings and controversy. He was too little of the partisan. The Whig interest in Norfolk, especially when it was in the doldrums, made tentative and half-hearted approaches to persuade him to become its candidate. Perhaps if they had unanimously assailed him, he might have consented. But the political interest of a county is rarely unanimous. Some Whigs were afraid that Boileau might not be acceptable to Coke; others that he would be unacceptable to Windham and his followers. The Church Whigs distrusted him because he wanted government help for Irish priests, the protection Whigs because he wanted free trade. He did not desire to be a politician, and took no steps whatever to secure the offer of a seat. He knew that even his speeches to the tenant-farmers limped from platitude to platitude. He could not see himself orating from a platform, and perhaps he thought such orating to be touched with vulgarity, to be unfitting.

He faithfully performed all the other duties of a magnate. He regularly attended the courts as a magistrate, he interested himself in the affairs of the police and the prison at Wymondham, he attended the judges when they came to the assize and offered them hospitality. He was a member of the committee of the hospital, and of the college for training teachers. He presided over the Norwich School of Design. He helped neighbours in trouble or in debt, he organized a county-wide collection for the relief of sufferers in the great storm of 1843, when the hail and the wind broke more than three hundred panes of glass at Ketteringham Hall. He frequently took the chair at local dinners, or the meetings of local societies. He performed these public functions dutifully, perhaps even enjoyed the prominence into which they brought him, but he performed them without self-confidence and with no real pleasure. He was nervous at public speaking, he never became eloquent.

He kept reminding himself of the disaster if the president broke down and always expected to break down. He would prepare his speeches with care, and then find his mind to be a blank. At the dinner of the Agricultural Society in 1844, 'I hardly knew what I said, felt I was not at all giving what I intended and knew not what would happen, but luckily having some short heads or notes I got some word idea, I know not how, back to my mind and from that moment all was again perfectly easy and I could have gone on for ever. As it was I did delay the meeting more than an hour — too long certainly — and good judgement would have made me cut half my matter out for another occasion — but the party was very kind and though somewhat showing signs of impatience at the extracts I read, they always got right again . . . always good-humoured and well taken.' He was much conscious of his inadequacies. Once at King's Lynn he had to follow Baron Alderson, and felt like a donkey aping a spaniel.

In 1844 he was high sheriff of the county. He had a special carriage made for him in London, with his arms emblazoned upon the doors; there were three banners to hang from his trumpets, each with the pelican in her piety and *De tout mon cœur*,[1] upon a background of yellow silk with a broad blue silk fringe. On 25th March, 1844, Judge Patteson came to Ketteringham for the sheriff's procession into Norwich. To the horror of the household he arrived nearly an hour early. No one was ready to receive him, Sir John was still out, Lady Catherine was beginning to dress, the children were out and the servants half-dressed. The judge was unperturbed; and after lunch set off in the sheriff's carriage with Sir John and the sheriff's chaplain and the judge's clerk. At the head went the marshal (Mr. Read) upon a grey horse, then the under-sheriff (Mr. Blake), then the outrider (Sir John's coachman), and then the coach with the four horses all grey, and two servants in livery in the rumble. All the servants were wearing immense yellow cockades. Sir John wore buckle shoes, white silk stockings, blue knee-breeches, a long waistcoat, a blue coat cut round, and

[1] Still dignified in their tatters, they are now in the possession of Mr. Bryan Hall of Banningham. They cost Sir John £10 for the three (Ama's diary, 16th March, 1844), which the family thought very little.

lace ruffles, like the old court dress of the time of George III. The buttons on the suit had been made for the famous Egalité Duke of Orleans and had been bought in Paris by Sir John's father; each button glittered with a set of imitation diamonds and topaz, and the relic was believed to be worth about 100 guineas. A small body of tenants and neighbours paid Sir John the compliment of riding after him. He had commanded all the villagers to assemble at the lodge gates to cheer him. Andrew saw him in Norwich and thought he looked a truly happy man. He observed however that the city sheriff's carriage far out-stripped Sir John's carriage. 'All is vanity,' he soliloquized.

Sir John went to London every year for the season. His family travelled with servants and luggage, and after the railway was built, occupied two first-class carriages, two second-class carriages, a truck, and a horse-box. Usually he left Ketteringham in March and returned in July. He lived during those months at his house in Upper Brook Street, and as his family grew up, the need to provide his daughters with dances and society and eligible young men, the need to present them at court, took an increasing proportion of his time in London. He did not always enjoy the round of parties, the same people talking about the same things, and once wrote of 'all my little nothings which make the great something of this life'. But he worked hard in London. Few men can have done so much useful service below the highest. He was upon the Westminster committee of the Great Exhibition of 1851. He diligently attended the committee of the Magdalen Hospital for the reclaiming of prostitutes, and the Mendicity Society (a most aristocratic committee) which relieved beggars. He obtained some pleasure at his association with the great ones of the land, from Lord John Russell downwards, but his chief interests were literary, artistic, scientific. He belonged to a generation which believed that a gentleman was not educated unless he was interested in literature, in art, in science. He was a member of all the great scientific societies, and on the committee of almost all of them. At various times he was vice-president of the Royal Society of Literature, the Zoological Society (the sites of the hippopotamus house and the giraffe house at the London Zoo were in part due to his interest), the Statistical Society, the British Association for the Advancement of Science, the Royal Institution. In June 1843, he was elected a Fellow of the Royal Society; in December 1852, a Fellow of the Society of Antiquaries. For a time he was chairman of the Fine Arts Committee of the Society of Arts. These offices give no indication of the amount of time which he spent in forwarding the interests of the diverse societies.

These interests brought him into association with the highest in the land — in literature, especially Hallam and Macaulay; in science, especially Owen, Faraday, Sedgwick, and Henslow. When Guizot was driven from the leadership of France by the Paris barricades of 1848, he found a temporary refuge through the kindness of Sir John Boileau, and that assistance cemented a lasting friendship between the two families. But Sir John always missed the highest. While Lord John Russell was Prime Minister, he found his patronage much sought, for Lady Catherine Boileau was sister to Lord John's wife. But after Russell had gone out of office, he was never near the inner councils of State. And this was true of his science and his literature. In 1860, the British Association for the Advancement of Science held their meeting in Oxford, that meeting where Bishop Wilberforce and Professor Huxley met in the collision over man's descent from apes, the noise of which would reverberate through the later nineteenth century. It is somehow characteristic of Sir John that he should have been staying for the meeting in Bishop Wilberforce's palace at Cuddesdon, but should have failed to attend that session.

He brought many of his eminent friends to stay at Ketteringham — Lord John Russell, Guizot, Bishop Stanley, Arthur Stanley, Lord Braybrooke, the historian Hallam, and a host of lesser lights. One lady from Norwich was a welcome and stimulating visitor, Amelia Opie. After the death of her husband, the painter, she had turned Quaker, and yet retained with her black bonnet and grey silks an air of attractive worldliness which led people to accuse her of insincerity. Distinguished as an authoress, as a person and as an intimate of the Gurney circle, she never ceased to give her friends, with her waggish face and twinkling eyes, the feeling that she might at once burst into a romp, a game perhaps of bo-peep. She brought into the austere atmosphere of Ketteringham Hall a breath of skittishness and archness and roguery which even Sir John never seems to have resented. It is safe to say that no one but Mrs. Opie could with impunity begin a letter to Sir John Boileau with the words 'O thou amiable thing!', or end with a postscript, 'a lump of love to distribute, Sir John — among thy belongings'.

Of these literary interests, the encouragement of the Norfolk Archaeological Society must be reckoned among the chief. He soon succeeded Bishop Stanley as president of the society. His notable act of service was the purchase of the ruins and site of Burgh Castle, important among the Roman sites of East Anglia — on 3rd September, 1846, he bought twenty-eight acres there for £1,500. As an investment in land this was poor: the agricultural part of the property yielded a very low return. It was an act of public spirit to preserve the ruin for archaeological inquiry. He went over to Burgh from time to time to encourage excavators or to interest his visitors.

*   *   *   *   *

Eighty years later, the interior of Ketteringham Hall was like an antique shop with an excess of furniture, some of it beautiful, too many pictures upon the walls, landscapes painted upon shells and dingy photographs and prints, red plush frames, a mustiness like the odour of old and little-used sofas, antlers and horns sprouting from the walls, oils and water-colours jumbled together, occasional tables covered in china and medallions and bric-à-brac; chosen apparently with so eclectic a taste that the visitor would need to push past some hideous lump of Victorian mahogany to see the most charming and delicate little object sheltering behind. Grim and serviceable table-cloths drooped over tables which, when unveiled, were seen to be exquisite representatives of French furniture, and the chairs and sofa in the drawing-room were covered with too lasting a mustard-and-green cretonne. In the corners were busts of distinguished men, there were marble statues, one or two of them lovely antiquities from Rome; in the corridors were glass cases exhibiting stuffed birds, on the staircase were men in armour, in the bedrooms were large fourposter beds of bright mahogany draped with heavy curtains.

Such was the furniture of Ketteringham Hall eighty years later. But the collection, or jumble, had grown over the years. It was not like this when Sir John returned from his continental tour and took up residence in 1841. Eighty years later a mood of conservatism prevailed at Ketteringham and any piece of cretonne gives forth mustiness if left long enough. It was true that the Roman statuary and carvings were mostly bought by Sir John at Nice during his continental tour and carried home among his possessions. It was true that he possessed an admirable collection of pictures — two van Goyens, a Reynolds, a Velazquez, a Jan van Eyck, paintings by Guido and Matsys, a Gainsborough sketch, the portrait of Rousseau by Wright of Derby, two little marble heads by Westmacott. But he kept these works not at Ketteringham, but at his London house, and only after his death were some of them moved to Ketteringham. In 1841 there were no photographs upon the walls of the Hall, or of anyone else's house. Many of the best portraits which afterwards came to Ketteringham arrived towards the end of the century, not from the Boileaus, but from the family of Sir John's daughter-in-law, Lucy Nugent. In 1841 most of the pictures on the walls at Ketteringham were still Atkyns pictures which had been thrown in when he bought the house. It was true that two immense wapiti horns were fixed to the walls of his new Gothick hall in the year 1845. These had not been shot in the chase, but were presented to him as a symbol of esteem by the London Zoo.

He was not an extravagant collector. He was acutely aware, all his later life, that he must provide for nine children. In London he would go into the auction rooms and watch the sales of painting or of silver, and sometimes, like other men, he would bid for what he never meant to buy and be vexed when an unwanted drawing was knocked down to him. But he would never bid excitingly. His duty to his children would keep thrusting itself into his conscience, and prevented him from being the collector which, in his quiet, amateur way, he was well qualified to become. When he bought, he would usually store or hang his acquisition at Upper Brook Street, where the world and his friends might admire it during the London season. The future clutter at Ketteringham had not yet become a clutter.

*　　*　　*　　*　　*

He who would understand Ketteringham must turn his eyes past the figure of the squire towards the wife sheltering behind him. The village never knew her well. She was often ill, always in retirement, shrinking from the public eye. When she was fit she would visit the sick and poor among the cottages. But she was a woman of the bedroom and the boudoir and her 'pit' in the garden, and came out little. Andrew believed that she was ruled absolutely by an imperious husband, and pitied her, and hardly knew her.

She is the most shadowy of all the Boileau household, the hardest to frame in history. She was a beautiful woman. She had a delicate, sensitive mouth, brown eyes, and lovely dark hair; and in both the Shee portrait and the Grant portrait affection and gentleness are unmistakable, and yet there is something more — perhaps an aura of withdrawal would best describe it.

She had been carefully brought up by her Minto parents. The books of her childhood which she passed to her eldest daughter included *The Spoiled Child; or Indulgence Counteracted*, by Mrs. Pilkington (1799), and *Henry: or The Foundling to which are added, The Prejudiced Parent; or The Victorious daughter — Tales calculated to improve the minds and morals of youth*, also by Mrs. Pilkington. Like so many of that age, she had learnt to keep a journal of reflections and self-examination, and some of these self-examinations have survived. She tried by this means to identify herself with her husband.

On 19th November, 1835, she wrote questions for self-examination every evening; and the mood in which these questions are framed bears upon the history of Ketteringham parish:

Have I been dutiful and affectionate in my manner, as well as in my feelings, towards my dear husband this day?

Have I listened to him when speaking to me, with *attention*, with a desire to understand his meaning, with a readiness to enter into his views, to agree with his opinions?

Have I guarded against my disposition to contradict and to find objections to what he says?

Have I taken care neither to be sulkily silent, or hasty in answering him, in conversation?

Have I submitted with a *cheerful humility* when he has thought right to reprove me for or point out any of my faults?

Have I resisted with all my strength all desire to *defend* myself even if I should have not seen my fault?

Have I felt *grateful* for his advice and admonition, and *tried sincerely* to believe his motive is to do me good?

Have I shewn myself ready to arrange my occupations to suit his hours and his convenience, and that without tormenting him with questions?

Have I tried in *everything* to consult his wishes?

Have I prayed earnestly for the assistance of God for my Saviour's sake, in all these duties *not relying* too much on my *own strength?*

She was sometimes frightened of him. He had been carefully brought up by an elderly father and had the highest regard for propriety. He was sensitive to roughness or aggressiveness in manner, and practised without effort the courtliness of an early Victorian gentleman. He was so meticulous that he could sometimes fuss. He was accustomed to record his expenditure, he examined his wife's accounts for housekeeping, he deplored extravagance, never failed to rebuke his servants for the least slovenliness or carelessness, and he personally audited the goods in his house down to the last teaspoon and the nursery plate.

She tried to persuade herself that this fear was wholesome. It worried her that he took so despondent a view of the conduct of his household, his children, his servants. She tried to stop herself resisting him, tried to stop herself defending them against his severity, but found it impossible. Rarely she used, unwittingly, the legendary armour of Victorian wives, tears and hysteria; but for the most part she tried to keep herself modest, and meek, and though keeping her opinion, not setting it up against his. As the children grew up, and the disagreement between the parents began to matter more, there were painful arguments in the bedroom, and occasionally even downstairs. 'It cannot lead to our happiness,' he told her, 'nor can it be right in you, when I am vexed with my son, to take his part and argue with me that I am wrong in my judgement of him. If you could *gently* and *respectfully* represent to me as your husband and his father that "perhaps he might have mistaken something" or that "perhaps something had been mistakenly told me" — *this* might do good and would be right in *you* — allowing the blame I found in my son, as I *saw* it, not thwarting *that*, or making yourself a better judge of facts than me — and at once opposing my opinion by yours as if I am judging harshly or wrongly — as you can only by this irritate my feelings more and excite also great apprehension that any child must perceive you opposing me and find therefore support for his own error — the result of course being dissension between father and mother, the child clinging to the one (who) supported him — and all getting wrong together.'

She was sometimes afflicted with despair. She would never please him, she thought (in her disloyal moments) that he must be prejudiced about the household. A modern doctor might guess that part of the cause of her long illnesses was the inescapable plight of being mistress of a household where the master set a standard of order so high as to be beyond her capacity.

Her conscience believed that her husband was right. It was her duty to be obedient, even when her heart wanted to rush to the children's aid. But the affections of the heart flowed too strongly and too rapidly to be dammed by the flimsy barrier of dutifulness. Her eldest daughter once compared her to the peahen on the Hall terrace, protecting its chicks. Her husband sometimes found her pertinacious.

Yet they remained deeply in love with each other. Her quiet, serene, meek beauty gave him peace. His manliness, and consistency, and determination, and principle, and courtesy held her, as once they had won her. No one who reads his descriptions of her last illness, or the little fragments of her papers which he wept over when she was gone, will doubt that they remained deeply in love with each other.

* * * * *

There is not enough evidence to determine whether the piety of the wife deepened the piety of the husband, or whether he was a devout man before he married. He first comes alive to the historian after he reached Ketteringham. He was accustomed to read prayers daily to his family, which included his servants as well as his children. In the afternoon of Sunday he would search to prepare a suitable sermon from the volumes of sermons upon his shelves, and would read it in the evening to his family — perhaps a sermon by Vaughan, or Kingsley, or Arnold, or Preston, or Pyle, or Cooper. (The informed will discern that, as he was a Whig in political allegiance, so he was a liberal in his choice of religious masters.) He prepared his footmen for confirmation, a process which consisted in hearing their catechism. He visited the poor, sat by the bedsides of the sick and prayed with them, paid wages to men who could not work so that they could be kept out of the workhouse, gave them coal at Christmas, promised prizes of five shillings to the mothers whose children went most regularly to school or to the women who knitted the best pair of worsted stockings. Every January he gave a dinner of roast beef and plum pudding and ale to the poor men of the parish; and at the dinner of 1844, for example, he addressed them for twenty minutes, pointing out the wisdom of checking idle or mischievous habits in time, praised their conduct generally, spoke of preserving game, improving gardens and cottages. When he found that his servants did not attend the Sacrament, he exhorted them or read to them until they were ready to attend — and when at last they came, he rejoiced.

He thus possessed a high sense of his pastoral vocation to the villagers of Ketteringham. The night when he arrived in Ketteringham after his continental tour, he said a prayer that he might be the father of the fatherless in the parish, the husband to the widow, a peace-maker and a teacher to the poor. He imagined himself to be 'the father of the parish', and used that phrase to describe himself. His ideals were best expressed in his record of the speech which he made to his tenants at the dinner to which he invited them on 13th February, 1854. 'I addressed them after on the comfort of living in Ketteringham, where they had a comfortable church — good school for the children — decent cottages and gardens at moderate rents or low ones — sure of being attended to if sick or find a friend if in want of one — and no man well-behaved out of employment at fair wages. Therefore they ought to be zealous, diligent, respectful workmen for their employers and kind to each other. Satisfied with their conduct on the whole, and thought them respectable but obliged to punish for the thefts committed this year, and they might be sure while desirous to encourage the good I must and would bring really bad conduct to punishment. Mr. Beck now in charge of the estate, a kind good man, but the rules for cottagers for not taking in lodgers etc. must be carefully kept by him.' It was no empty word to say that he was the father of the parish. He built lodges at the entrances to the park, cottages for his labourers and houses for his tenant-farmers, and took trouble in teaching his tenants how to keep them neat and clean.

Tucked incongruously among a bundle of his estimates for the alterations to the Hall, is docketed a most characteristic document. It is headed *Pros and cons for going abroad, 1846-7.* Both the advantages upon the left page, and the disadvantages upon the right page tell something about the man. By going abroad, he would save about £4,000, he would save the expense of making further improvements to the Hall, he would avoid elections and all their worst consequences, he would reduce some part of his establishment; the girls would learn languages, his wife and his daughter Carry would gain in health. To the contrary, he feared to unsettle the habits of his family, and either to leave the boys in England or to interrupt their education; he thought it wrong to desert the poor of Ketteringham on the one hand, and the wealthy London society on the other; and the list of disadvantages ends with a laconic but not too mysterious note: 'place left — Mr. A.'.

His conduct during a local strike illustrates both the man and his time. The winter of 1847 was hard for the poor, not as hard in England as in Ireland, but still a time of unemployment and near-famine. He helped the poor in his own parish with a little extra coal at Christmas, and with a distribution of tea and sugar. On 4th May[1] he received an urgent message requesting him to go over to the Union because the men of three parishes had struck work for higher wages and were compelling others to join them. He drove over in the phaeton with Easton his gardener, and found about 100 men assembled in the road outside the gate, and watched by police. He addressed himself to their spokesman, who seemed a sensible, steady, well-mannered fellow. 'I felt very kindly,' wrote Sir John, 'towards this manly specimen of a British peasant.' The spokesman asked that the Board of Guardians should fix a higher wage. Sir John kindly explained that a Board of Guardians or a Board of Magistrates could not fix a wage; that a wage was an agreement

[1] I have in my possession an autograph letter from Bishop Stanley of Norwich to Sir Denis le Marchant at the Home Office, asking for a military detachment to reinforce the police during these troubles.

between man and man; that he (the spokesman) would not like magistrates or boards to have power to make him pay for his loaf of bread whatever the baker chose to ask, though it were double the market price; and therefore there ought to be no similar power to make an employer pay him or any other labourer the price at which he or others might choose to value their labour.

The spokesman seemed to understand the explanation, and thanked Sir John; who added, 'It is my own feeling and opinion that wages ought to be raised to keep pace with the great rise in the price of provisions.' He said that he had raised the wages of his own workmen only two days ago. 'I firmly believe that the same right spirit will be found in the farmers and other employers if you go each to your own master and respectfully and properly show your case. But assembling together to obtain your object by intimidation or by stopping others from work cannot be allowed and you will get into trouble. I advise you to go and say this to your companions.'

The man went out respectfully to the crowd at the gate. Sir John turned to the members of the Board and urged them strongly to raise the wages. He went out of the gate, called the men round him, sent the police away, and advised them to go home and speak properly to their masters. Sixty or seventy men went away. The twenty-five or thirty who remained seemed to him sulkily disposed, and he warned them seriously. When he went away he persuaded friends whom he met to raise their wages; he gave Andrew £5 to distribute to the needy in the village; and he asked the police superintendent to give him a man to guard his barn from robbers.

It was natural that such a man, liked by his equals, should be feared as much as liked by his parishioners. As the father of his parish, he saw it to be his immediate duty to ensure the good behaviour of its residents. (In the Swing riots of 1830 a rough near Walsingham had declared that Boileau was 'a great man for putting people in gaol' and had better 'look to himself'). When he met a waggon and horses driven furiously upon the public highway, he turned his horse and galloped after it and forced the driver to stop. He occasionally whipped boys in the village for misconduct or impertinence. When a rude boy shouted at him while he was out riding, he reined his horse and lectured the boy into silence. When he found an unauthorized pony and cart tied to his gate, he untied it and turned it loose. Servants who misbehaved might find themselves held up to public opprobrium in the exhortation after family prayers, and grievous offenders were excluded from the prayers. He preferred respectable tenants to high rents, and would not allow dissenters among his tenants. Osborne's boy was guilty of an offence like robbing the squire's orchard of its apples; Osborne was ordered to bring the boy down to the Hall and flog him there; he came, but refused to flog, and had to be carried before the magistrates. Goutry, who was reported to have grumbled that his sheep had been put into a place with scabby sheep of Sir John's, found his rent raised by £1 per annum. Occasionally Sir John expelled a man or woman from the village for immoral behaviour, and more often used the threat to expel. Sometimes he was unpopular upon a matter of high principle. He would not employ boys under the age of twelve, nor then unless they had remained at school till the age of twelve; and this admirable principle was resented in the village. In 1851, he received an anonymous letter threatening to kill him and burn down the Hall unless he raised his wages from 8s., and accusing him of being the first to separate men and women at the workhouse.

*　　*　　*　　*　　*

It was a paternal government. And within the parish, the vicar was a morsel undigested, an intrusive power. He represented a different influence upon the parishioners, an influence which could not always be controlled and was often unpredictable. Had Sir John Boileau been born a medieval king, he would have upheld the Byzantine system of church government, and fought the pretensions of archbishops to his last breath.

V

THE SUBMISSION OF THE CLERGY

SIR JOHN returned from his continental tour of 1839 to 1841 and was ready to be friendly with the vicar. He believed that the religious instruction of his parishioners was essential to their behaviour in this world and their welfare in the next, and looked to the vicar for due assistance in that instruction. His impression of the Andrews was friendly and favourable. He thought that Andrew conducted the wedding of his tutor and governess with reverence and simplicity; on 25th July, he heard Andrew preach an excellent sermon on the duties of servants and master; he was pleased that Andrew was not rigid to insist upon the catechism being taught to all the children in the village school. Now that he was back in England and expected to be living at Ketteringham for the greater part of each year, he wished to make alterations to the church. He wanted to build a gallery, to remove the school children from the body of the church, and to make the pews for the squire and his family more dignified and suitable. He discussed these plans with Andrew, and found him rational, pleasant, and submissive. He altered his own pew, and his servants' pew, provided curtains and whitened the walls of the church. The cost of erecting the gallery was estimated at £35. The visitor to Ketteringham church henceforth could not help seeing — and cannot help seeing today — a prominent inscription in capital letters across the front of the gallery: ERECTED SEPTEMBER 26TH, 1841, BY SIR JOHN P. BOILEAU, BART. It was the Victorian version of Sir Henry Grey's portrait in the east window. Sir Henry's portrait had dominated the congregation as they walked in. Sir John's inscription dominated them as they walked out.

He failed to realize that the struggle for a parsonage had left a scar upon Andrew and a deeper scar upon Mrs. Andrew; scars of mistrust. It seemed to them that the squire's actions over the house had been underhand. They were sure that he wished to drive them away, and they disliked the method. Some of the mistrust for the squire spilled over into the relationship with Bishop Stanley. For a time Andrew could hardly accept the squire's kindness without thinking it a Trojan horse. Whenever Sir John was particularly courteous, he suspected a plan which boded ill. If the Boileaus left Ketteringham by coincidence on the day he returned to it, he was ready to suspect that this was no coincidence. If Sir John expressed sympathy, he believed it to be feigned. He thought that the squire had been guilty of satanic craft, that the Boileau motto *De tout mon cœur* was not rightly emblazoned upon the arms of so insincere a man. And Sir John's first actions in the parish, which seemed to take no notice of Andrew's wishes or rights in the church, and to imply an assumption of absolute authority, convinced Andrew that his opinion was correct. Sir John, though he came to church regularly, was a hinderer of God's word. On 2nd November, 1841, Andrew added to his prayers this petition: 'My God and my Lord, humble this proud tyrant by the rod of thy all-subduing grace. Psalm xxxv.'

Sir John's diary shows that at this time he was altogether unaware of the tempests raging within Andrew and his wife. Ellen Andrew, it was true, found her sentiments more difficult to conceal and on one occasion was but distantly civil to Sir John's greeting. But Sir John at first liked most of the sermons under which he sat Sunday by Sunday, and found Andrew an easy man, obviously a sincere pastor with the interests of the parish at heart. He was not aware that his acts in the church, like erecting a monument to his deceased butler without telling the vicar, might be regarded as discourtesy or as trampling upon the vicar's rights. He was not aware that the vicar could be regarded as possessing any rights outside the conduct of the services. Not for four years did he realize how bitterly Andrew, and still more bitterly Mrs. Andrew, felt his despotic rule over Ketteringham church; and then only because Mrs. Andrew could bear no longer to hold her peace. He could not say that his judgment of Andrew was high. He soon formed the opinion that Bishop Stanley had been mistaken in appointing Andrew to be the rural dean of Humbleyard. He thought that his person and manner and conduct were in some ways peculiar, and discussed them with the bishop on more than one occasion. But he had no notion what deep-seated distrust and emotion his own acts had created in Andrew's breast.

The act which most distressed Andrew was the closing of the schoolroom against him.

*   *   *   *   *

A new school was needed at Ketteringham. It had been planned by the Atkyns family and Sir John interested himself in it as soon as he arrived in Norfolk. Various people, including Miss Atkyns, wished to contribute to the building fund. Sir John generously insisted on paying for the entire building from his own purse. When the school was built, he felt a natural and proprietary interest in its use and its welfare. It was opened on 28th January, 1840, under the charge of a girl named Sarah Cooper, who had been trained for this purpose in the school at Wymondham. Sir John paid her wages.

When the school was opened, Sir John was away upon his continental tour. Andrew believed that he had the right to occupy the school for his own meetings. He used it as a kind of parish hall. He began a course of lectures; and on 3rd December, 1840, the schoolroom witnessed an astonishing scene.

A labourer in the parish named Lightwing, who in 1838 had almost cut off his hand and in February, 1839, had broken his leg, suffered from mental depression; in the autumn of 1840 this passed over the brink into religious mania. Andrew first knew of it when his old clerk came and exclaimed exultingly, 'O, dear sir, poor Lightwing's soul is set at liberty!' Lightwing came to the vestry with a letter of four pages, wishing his religious experience to be declared from the pulpit. Andrew declared nothing of the kind from the pulpit and sent a notice to the overseers that Lightwing should be confined. At dawn on Monday morning an excited Lightwing came round to Wood Hall wishing to see the vicar. Mrs. Andrew was frightened of him, and would not trust them together; but Lightwing stayed for family prayers and for breakfast with the servants. He expressed surprise that Andrew had not read the letter from the pulpit, and said that he had got a barber at Wymondham to write the letter for him. He had bet the barber three sovereigns that the vicar would mention his name in his Sunday's sermon.

About two o'clock Mr. Barnard and Copeman drove up to Wood Hall in a cart, with Lightwing running wildly by its side. He had a chain in one hand as though they had failed in an attempt to secure his wrists. Andrew had gone away to his lecture at Ketteringham schoolroom; and while Barnard and Copeman hurried Mrs. Andrew and the two little children from the garden into the house, Lightwing stood outside, abusing the vicar and threatening that he would find him. Hearing that Andrew was in Ketteringham schoolroom, Lightwing set off thither, followed by Barnard and Copeman. Barnard sent a message ahead to the schoolroom to give warning.

Andrew was summoned to the door of the schoolroom and told, 'Lightwing is coming and is very angry with you, and Mr. Barnard hopes you will not come out of the room.' Andrew locked the door, and had the windows shut, and continued his lecture quietly, though he could hear Lightwing outside. At the end of the lecture he said: 'We cannot conclude with the Doxology. I have a reason for it.' He said a prayer, and as the people began to drift away, he begged them to wait a few minutes and then explained the circumstances. They kept the door locked and from the window watched Lightwing standing sentinel at the school gateway. Andrew described his escape thus: 'I sent out the woman Horstead who knew him well, hoping she could entice him toward the east end of the school whilst I fled from the west door; but he was too crafty. A window was now opened for me to leap out, but it was found scarcely practicable. I concealed myself under the window lest he should look in at the window. In a short time, finding that he was leaning upon the post at the entrance of the playground on the south side, I opened the door at the west end and ran as if for my life across the wheat on the north side, aiming as much as possible to keep the school as a screen; and providentially the poor fellow did not move from the gate till I had burst through the thorn hedge at the top of the field; when, exhausted, I turned and looked through the fence; but recollecting that he might have seen me and was making his way to meet me by another direction, I again started; and now he might have seen me from the school, but being carefully occupied in searching for me among the congregation he did not look in the direction I had taken. Having reached Mr. Radcliffe's at the Farm

House, I threw myself on the sofa; for my lungs being heated from exhortation and so suddenly and fully inflated with wintry air, I suffered much pain, but a little peppermint relieved me. In a little time Copeman brought the pony and gig with Mrs. Heazell saying that Lightwing had gone across a turnip field in a different direction, declaring that I had escaped in woman's clothes . . . I feel perfectly easy. O Lord, be thou my shield!'

Sarah Cooper, the schoolmistress, was a devout girl, a faithful pupil of the vicar. He was delighted that she had charge of the school and had every confidence in her, took her on holiday to Gorleston with Mrs. Tufts, his washerwoman, and was confirmed in his opinion of her when her children outstripped the children of neighbouring villages. From the day of opening the vicar was a little nervous whether someone whom he regarded as 'very suitable' would be thought suitable by the squire. Sir John, it was plain, regarded the school as his school. He owned the ground, had paid for the building, and was paying the stipend of the schoolmistress. His sense of possession was soon demonstrated.

Among his new decorations of the church had been a whitening of the walls. On 16th October, 1841, a Saturday evening, Sarah Cooper arrived at the vicarage to say that the painting in the church rendered services impossible there on the morrow. The news took Andrew by surprise. He told her that they would hold their Sunday service at half-past two in the schoolroom. When he arrived at the schoolroom he found an angry squire. Sir John, it seemed, thought that the schoolroom ought not to be used for such a purpose. On Monday, Andrew received a letter from Sir John stating that he would rather that the schoolroom should never be used without his concurrence. It appeared that he was troubled by more than this unexpected use. He had observed the usual strangers from other parishes at the service. And although he could not prevent the vicar allowing strangers into the parish church, he felt that he was failing in his duty if strangers were allowed to fill *his* schoolroom. Andrew was suffering grievously that night from cramp in the stomach. He viewed this contention with disfavour. On Wednesday, he received a letter reinforcing the letter of Monday. Sir John no longer said he 'would rather'; he plainly refused to permit the schoolroom to be used without his sanction.

For Sir John held it as a point of principle that a man should worship in his own parish church. In obedience to this duty he attended the morning service at Ketteringham church on every Sunday when he was in residence at the Hall. Even though in later years he resented the sermon, even though he believed the sermon erroneous in doctrine, even though he thought that a personal attack upon himself had been launched from the pulpit, even though he was bored unutterably, he still continued to attend morning service. With the exception of two Sundays when for a special reason (of which more later) he wondered whether he should go, and a few Sundays when he was not well enough to go, it never occurred to him that he should not be in his pew on Sunday morning. He would as soon have thought of neglecting to wash. For twenty-seven years he continued to sit under sermons many of which bored him, some of which distracted him, and some of which he wished to controvert.

He saw little distinction between a parishioner refusing to attend his church because he preferred the Methodist chapel and a parishioner refusing to attend his parish church because he preferred the preaching in a parish church three miles away. In both cases, Sir John felt, there was something schismatic. This was what lay under his question, when the bishop had been dining at the Hall, whether they could not drive away the strangers from Ketteringham church to make room for the villagers of Ketteringham. To Andrew this viewpoint was not intelligible. There was a Gospel to be preached and souls to be saved. If hungry sheep looked up in their own pastures and were not fed, how should he close the gates to them when they wandered into his pasture? If someone came into pastoral communion with Andrew, he sought them out in their own homes and prayed with them, even if those homes were outside the limits of his parish. If the vicar of a neighbouring parish failed altogether to shepherd an outlying community, Andrew had no sense that the geographical boundary of the parishes might prevent him from doing what he could for the community. There was an awkward meeting in the house of Mr. and Mrs. Tufts of Hethel, who had long been devout adherents of Andrew's ministry. Andrew walked through deep snow to read over his exposition of the Sunday to Mr. Tufts, who was too ill to come to church and whose wife was his washerwoman. The curate of Hethel, Mr. Fisher, entered in the middle to tell Tufts that coals would be given away. The two pastors shook hands and Andrew said cheerfully, 'I just came, Mr. Fisher, to see my poor patient.' Fisher was good-tempered; but Andrew felt more uneasy than he admitted, and knew that Fisher had easy access both to Sir John and to the bishop. He wished that he met Fisher less often. 'I never come into his parish,' he thought 'but that I stumble upon him.' His relations with the neighbouring rector, Mr. Day of Hethersett, were sometimes uncomfortable for the same reason. But no uneasy sense that others thought him a trespasser prevented Andrew from doing what he believed right. He was sure that he was no trespasser but was doing the Lord's work. There was often no one else to do it. On Wymondham Common, outside his parish, was a group of outlying families, unemployed and destitute labourers, gypsies and vagabonds. Andrew was in the habit of ministering to them as to his own parishioners; distributing soup (on one occasion 324 pints), clothes, fuel, mutton, potatoes, bottles of beer, blancmange, cough mixture, plaster, pills — all out of his own pocket; doctoring them in their epidemics; 'employing' their lads at 6d. each to learn the first chapter of the Epistle of St. James; correcting their errors when an itinerant American hot-gospelled among them. He could not bear it, when, as it seemed to him, some soul in need was being neglected. Mr. Cutmore, a grocer from London who had retired to Hethersett, cut his throat apparently for no better reason than biliousness and the purchase of some short-weight goods in Norwich. Day, his rector, did not visit his widow: Andrew, not his vicar, did.

He was sometimes inclined to chafe under the strings which church organization placed upon him. Once he caught himself wondering whether he would not be able to do more good outside the church. At least there were no squires and no parochial boundaries among the dissenters. He paid an occasional subscription to support the Moravians. But he was not friendly to dissent as dissent. The only dissent in his neighbourhood was Methodist or Ranting; he condemned the Methodists because they controverted Calvinism, and the Ranters because they ranted. He was inclined to think that all dissent was touched by vulgarity. But he would cheerfully attend a meeting at a nonconformist chapel and speak if he thought the cause good.

Sir John did not approve of this laxity. Like Andrew, he was a man to carry his principles into effective action. He discovered that a number of persons, not resident in Ketteringham parish, were using the footpaths through his park to attend the services at Ketteringham church. The church was easy of access from Hethersett. In other directions it was almost surrounded by the park, and those who came from the south would need to go several miles round unless they went through the park. Sir John took steps to discourage them. He closed the park, and so forced anyone thus disloyal to make a wearisome detour. Mrs. Tufts, the washerwoman, had not strength conveniently to encompass the walk. The vicar, feeling that relations between himself and his squire were complex, asked Ellen to write a letter requesting permission for Mrs. Tufts to cross the park. Sir John replied that he would personally see Mrs. Tufts. He sent for her (on Thursday, 26th October, 1843) and reproved her for not worshipping in her own parish church. He then said that he would give her permission to use the path through the park if she would bring a note from Mr. Fisher, her curate, saying that he might give her permission. Mrs. Tufts said that she could not do this. Sir John poured further reproaches upon her head, and ended the interview by presenting her with a brace of rabbits.

He could not stop strangers deserting their own parish churches and attending Ketteringham church otherwise than by forcing them to a journey of several miles. But the school was his school, and he could prevent it being used for purposes which he could not support. He professed himself ready, and indeed he was ready, to listen sympathetically to any applications which Andrew might make for the use of the school. But it was not surprising that Andrew made few applications. The vicar found himself, in effect, deprived of the use of the parish hall.

By way of illustration, Andrew once wrote a letter to Sir John asking if he might use the schoolroom to give instruction to the confirmed. He received in reply a note which gave him the permission. Upon a lovely spring evening Sir John was strolling through the park, and met Mr. and Mrs. Andrew driving along in a gig, with a large black setter gambolling about the grounds upon either side of the road. The setter sprang two pair of birds close to Sir John and, while he conversed with the Andrews, dashed into Furze Covert, worried a hare out and chased it across to Home Wood. Sir John politely remonstrated with Andrew for allowing the dog and begged him in future to tie it under the gig. Mr. Andrew asked, at this unpropitious moment, about the use of the schoolroom.

'To what *extent* may I use it?' asked Andrew.

'To the extent you asked for.'

'If I wished to collect a few people at any time?'

'If for a missionary meeting,' said Sir John, 'or anything I do not quite agree with you on, I could not lend it, as it would make me appear to join in that I do not wish.'

Mrs. Andrew broke in imperiously.

'Missionary meeting! We will take the church then if we want it.'

'Pray, Mrs. Andrew,' said Sir John, 'allow me to speak to Mr. Andrew.'

'May I,' asked Andrew perseveringly, 'use it to give a lecture on the Scriptures if I had an hour of an evening?'

'Certainly, if to the parish.'

'I cannot say if others might not come. I cannot keep them away.'

'I could not wish to bring strangers into the parish, but for the people of it you would always be welcome. But if you will let me know beforehand, I have no doubt we shall arrange it.'

Mrs. Andrew began to talk about 'assisting everyone to hear the Scriptures,' but at this moment the dog was observed in full cry after another quarry, and the gig drove in pursuit, perhaps shamefacedly.

*   *   *   *   *

Little Sarah Cooper, the schoolmistress, soon found herself in an embarrassing predicament. She was Mr. Andrew's protégée and disciple. She had been appointed under his influence, had been taught by him and encouraged by him. She admired him, and wished to conduct the school on principles which he approved. But she was also Sir John's schoolmistress, teaching in Sir John's building, dependent upon him for her daily bread, a servant no more free of his control than his butler or his gardener.

On the eve of 1842, Sir John gave a ball for all his servants. He described it in his diary.

'Dined early, and in evening servants had a ball in the hall, lighted up. There were our ten maids — four indoor and three outdoor, and Cowper — Easton and three gardeners there, besides John Cannell and wife, Mr. and Mrs. Smith and Lutman — Sarah Cooper — Betsy Mumford and Fisher the carpenter — thirty — and the children. It went off well as they had a supper also, and all over by two o'clock, which was somewhat too late. I took Mrs. Beale to dance in the New Year but she was puffy and obliged to sit down.'

Andrew disapproved of these proceedings,[1] and hoped that some of the participants also disapproved. He found villagers like Jonas Horstead, the fiddler, who professed uneasy conscience but nevertheless had attended the ball. He was grieved when he found that Sarah Cooper was among them. When he expressed his grief, Sarah said, 'I was miserable all the while and always wished from the first not to have anything to do with the school under Sir John. But he came to me saying, "I know Mr. Andrew does not agree with me that balls are not wrong. I see no wrong and I myself join in the dance. Besides, remember you are now my schoolmistress, not his!" ' This at least was Sarah's account of her fall, and Andrew found it impossible to be cross with one so penitent and unhappy. He

---

[1] The attitude of Andrew and his friends to dancing was succinctly put in a conversation between his neighbour, Archdeacon Philpot, and the squire of Clermont.

Lady Goodricke (who was on Philpot's side): I suppose, Mr. Philpot, you are not going to take your daughters to the Coursing Ball at Swaffham tomorrow evening?

Philpot: No, Lady Goodricke, I don't approve of such amusements for young ladies.

Sir Francis Goodricke (somewhat sharply): What's your objection, sir?

Philpot: Well, Sir Francis, they have all been *baptised*, and at their *baptism* it was promised in their name they should renounce the pomp and vanities of this *world* — and if you don't find the *world* in a ballroom, where would you look for it?

bore his testimony against the pomps and vanities of the world, and took his leave.

The next year (1843) at New Year's tide, Andrew was away from Ketteringham upon a long recuperative holiday. In the New Year of 1844, Sir John again invited his servants to a ball. Sarah Cooper came to consult the vicar whether she should go. She must have known the answer before she asked the question. He laid before her 'what the Word of God says', and left it to her to choose; and advised her to give no reasons for not going until after the ball; if she were then asked why she had not gone, she should say that she could not conscientiously join in these pleasures, and especially that she would not be able to reprove the children. Sarah obeyed the advice apart from the last, difficult, test. Miss Caroline Boileau asked her why she was not present. 'I was not well,' said Sarah Cooper. It was true. The vicar thought it nevertheless to be the answer of a faint heart.

On New Year's Eve, 1845, Sir John observed that Sarah could not attend the servants' ball because she was taking the children to the Andrews' house.

The predicament of Sarah Cooper, though acute, represented a problem which slowly began to afflict many in the parish. It was a conflict of loyalties. In a little parish of 200 souls, where everyone was a servant of the squire, a growing breach between squire and parson could tear the parish asunder. And this conflict of loyalties would grow, like a seed growing secretly, until it penetrated into the bedrooms of Ketteringham Hall, into the heart of Sir John's family life.

* * * * *

The inhabitants of Ketteringham and the surrounding villages were rustic. Even superstition and witchcraft flickered amidst the flames on their hearths.

In the parish of Bracon Ash, Mr. Bickmore found a woman who intended to draw blood with a cut from her son's ear and with it make the sign of the cross on his breast to cure him of an improper growth of his shoulders and body. A man of Mulbarton, believing that four of his ducks were bewitched because they were not fattening quickly, asked his wife to roast one of the ducks in the hottest oven, to expel the witchery from the other three. Some of them would not use green elder among the firewood, because they believed that ague would surely come into the house where green elder was burnt. On 26th September, 1846, Rebecca Derham admitted wounding Mary Wickham's arm with a knife and professed herself ready to suffer any penalty which petty sessions might impose, because she had cured herself of pains and aches by drawing blood from Mary Wickham, who was a witch. Old Mrs. Durrant, who lived in one of the Ketteringham cottages, had heard in her young days that the streets of London were paved with gold, and had made a journey with her first husband in the hope of getting some. When the Maynooth grant was deliberated, and it was rumoured that the Roman Catholics were gaining in power, James Bird of Cressingham told his vicar, 'Sir, if them there Papishers come here, I have loosed one of the bricks in my cottage floor where I can hide my Bible that they can't find it.'

On 27th April, 1847, Lady Catherine Boileau was out walking in the village with her daughter Agnes and met Mrs. Durrant. She asked after her rheumatism, and then Mrs. Durrant exclaimed in a voice of lamentation, 'What a *sad* thing this is, is it not, my Lady? Is it not *dreadful*?'

'What thing?''

'Why sure have you not heard, my Lady? I mean about the children being killed?'

'No,' said Lady Catherine. 'What children? and how?' She supposed that some accident must have happened.

'O dear, I *wonder* you have not *heard*, that the Queen has ordered all the children in the kingdom under five years of age to be killed.'

Lady Catherine wanted to laugh; but Mrs. Durrant looked so unhappy and so serious that she could not. She tried to explain that the Queen had no power to order such a thing even if she wished it, but that she was a good and kind woman and never would wish it. She went into all the cottages and found everyone else, except the sceptical Mrs. Thrower, believing the report. Some said they hardly knew how to believe it — especially as it was said the Queen was to begin by two of her own children — but then, as they were *dumb* and had not their right know (i.e. were idiots) she did not perhaps mind so much. Upon inquiry the Boileaus found that this idea of Queen Victoria as a modern Herod was widely believed in Hethersett and other neighbouring villages. It appeared to have arisen because the Poor Law authorities had issued a decree that all the children in the poor house should be vaccinated.

In those days countrymen were still countrymen. And being thus simple, they were distressed by the evident conflict between squire and vicar, both of whom they respected. If the squire and the vicar were a little afraid of each other, the cottagers were more than a little afraid of both. Some took sides; and there began even to be two factions among them. 'The parish,' confessed Andrew in January 1844, 'is divided between Sir John's favourites and ours.' Sir John would wander among the cottagers and be outspoken against the strangers who attended Ketteringham church. On 8th June 1845, Andrew went down to Mr. Clark's cottage to join a singing party. He found that the people, in their fear of Sir John, were embarrassed to receive him into the cottage and he was therefore forced to invite the whole party to his own house. Sir John, perceiving the factions and worrying over them, proposed to Andrew that they should make a display of their unity by jointly visiting the cottages. He suggested also that they should join in distributing potatoes to the poor. Andrew refused. He believed that any such public show would be a deceit. There were differences of principle between them and it did not help the villagers to be confused about their choice of principle or to suppose that the different principles were equally good. The refusal did not encourage the squire to look with favour upon his vicar.

We must try to diagnose the reasons for the widening chasm between two good men.

Upon Andrew's side, the diagnosis is simple. The squire had tried to rob him of his house, and he was married to a wife who could hardly forget it. Accustomed to rule the parish before Sir John arrived, he now found everything taken out of his hands, from the use of the schoolroom downwards. A monument was erected upon the church wall, another monument (one of those to a member of the Atkyns family) was moved and a new monument put in its place, and all without reference to Andrew, who first discovered these changes when he entered the church to conduct services. Andrew could not believe (what was the truth) that Sir John never imagined the vicar to have more right in the matter than his schoolmistress. Sir John would no more have thought of asking Andrew's permission to hang a monument on the wall of *his* church than of asking his permission to hang a picture on the wall of his drawing-room. Andrew never supposed that this was Sir John's belief. He thought that Sir John must be aware of his rights and was consciously trampling upon them. He believed that these pinpricks were intended to harass. He ascribed them to malice, not to ignorance.

In the late summer of 1845, Sir John, at his own expense, and without informing the vicar, pulled down a hot-water pipe from the church and made building alterations to the vestry. It seemed to Ellen Andrew the last straw. She could not hold her peace.

Ellen Andrew to Sir John Boileau, 2nd September, 1845:
Dear Sir John,
   It is a subject of surprise that such frequent alterations should take place in our church without any reference to my husband who as a matter of right as well as a courtesy, should be consulted in any change about to be made, but an alteration *specially* concerning myself, induces me now to address you with that candour that should characterize professing Christians; the vestry where we live the greater portion of the Sundays in the year has been intruded on, and the room which was always too small, has been made smaller still by your order, and I appeal to you whether the act is consistent with that union that should exist between the Minister and the principal inhabitant of the parish. I pass by many other things that I could mention but it is our desire 'as much as in us lies to live peaceably with all men'. You know too well with what earnestness my dear husband seeks the salvation of souls, and that he opposes not your will in any mere temporal matter and this may account for his silence at all times on such subjects. I agree with his determination but at the same time I think you ought to be aware that we have *both some feeling* and that we understand the courtesies of life.
   — Believe me to remain, dear Sir John,
                    Faithfully yours,
                                   ELLEN ANDREW

Sir John Boileau to the Reverend W. W. Andrew, 3rd September, 1845:
Dear Sir,

I beg to enclose you a copy of a note I have this morning received from Mrs. Andrew, and I think you have either not seen it or forgotten our late interview in Ketteringham church when we talked over the alteration proposed to the entrance to the chancel and my pew. Mrs. A. writes in so excited a tone that I am persuaded you will make my excuses to her for not answering directly to herself — but if you have anything which you wish to say to me I shall be happy to hear from you and give it my best attention.

I am, dear sir,
Faithfully yours,
J. P. Boileau

On 22nd September, even Andrew, frightened though he was of Sir John, ventured a verbal protest about the vestry.

'I have a right,' said Sir John, 'to pull it down if I please.' Andrew understood him to threaten to do so if he was thwarted.

'I doubt of your right in the matter,' he said.

They argued over it. Andrew said how important it was for himself as a minister to act consistently.

'I cannot see', said Sir John, 'that your conduct is at all more important than mine. I am as answerable for the souls of my parish as you are. There is not the least difference in our situations except that I cannot perform the services of the church.'

Andrew felt nevertheless that the little explosion had done good. His friend Sharpe referred whimsically to the squire as Sir John Boil-over. But Andrew resolved for the future 'to go to him on every occasion with the utmost frankness whether for reproof or petition'. He found the resolution easier to break than to keep. On 2nd August, 1846, he observed Sir John and Lady Catherine laughing in their pew during service. He doubtless remembered how boldly he had rebuked Squire Ogilby for the same offence. Out visiting the following Wednesday, he met Sir John and Lady Catherine, but the moment did not seem opportune for rebuking them. 'I must do it!' he exhorted himself. It does not seem that he kept the resolution. He consulted his friend Leaward in Norwich. Leaward advised that if he saw them laughing he should stop the service and look earnestly towards the squire's pew.[1]

Sir John's motives for discontent with Andrew were more complicated. Andrew failed to fit Sir John's conception of the parish system. Sir John disapproved of other clergymen who were too sycophantic to their squires. When Mr. Bickmore went away to a parish and became 'a tame cat' to his squire, Sir John was contemptuous. But in Ketteringham, Andrew fitted his scheme of things too little. If Andrew had been a nonentity, or had preached sermons without bite, or had emptied the church, or had sent his congregation to sleep, or had had no disciples, it might have been easier. The squire would have effectually prevented the church being emptied. He not only took his own household, but brought pressure to bear upon his tenants, a pressure which could be resisted only upon the plea of ill-health. The cottagers, on the whole, went to church. And yet he was ensuring that Sunday by Sunday they received instruction from a man whose sermons he often disapproved, who was impossible to disregard or neglect, whether he was in or out of a pulpit. By an irony of events he lay under the moral obligation to influence his people to sit at the feet of a powerful teacher whose influence he distrusted. He never questioned this obligation.

Andrew was an enthusiast in the best and worst sense of that term. He had no reading but his Bible, or books directed to the understanding of the Bible. He had no interests outside his parish, no hobbies but gardening, and in these years he had twinges of conscience about gardening. If he went out for an afternoon's walk he took a bundle of tracts in his pocket and distributed them to travellers along the Norwich to Wymondham road. If he found that riders or drivers hurried their horses to avoid his offerings, he would cut a cleft in a long stick, fix a tract in the cleft, and hold it high in the road for the horseman to snatch as he galloped by. If he took a journey by the new railway line, opened in 1845, he devoted the time to a ministry

[1] Some years before, there had been an unseemly wrangle at Intwood church nearby. Mr. Smith, the clergyman, stopped the service and said to Mr. Alderton, 'Sir, you are laughing. Clerk, turn that man out!' Mr. Alderton stood his ground, and the result was not edifying.

among his fellow-passengers, the porters, or the ticket-collector. Almost every September he took his growing family away to holiday at Gorleston on the coast; but while his family played, he was cultivating a widespread circle of friends among the fishermen and the crews of the trawlers, and exercising a ministry among them. He had an exceptional capacity for preaching the Gospel out of season as well as in season; though it would be truer to say that he had no consciousness of any time which could be called 'out of season'.

In the pulpit, therefore, he poured forth fruits of his meditations. His sermons were not short. As one of his New Year resolutions for 1844, he determined to preach for half an hour only. He found the resolution impossible to keep. A prepared sermon of 65 minutes is recorded, and when he preached extempore, it might well be longer. (A friend once reminded him of the riddle, 'Why is an extempore sermon like a ring?' 'Because it is endless.' 'You preached for an hour and a quarter.') His head was full of the Bible and highly organized exegesis of the Bible, and it flowed from him like a fountain of waters. And if his hearers found the matter dull, they could not avoid noticing his manner. He leapt energetically about the pulpit, repeated sentences with strange emphases that sometimes bore no apparent relation to the sense, believed passionately in what he was saying and sought to communicate the passion. In neither of his moods did Sir John enjoy the sermon. Sometimes Sir John found it tedious, prosy, drawling, repetitive, heavy, rambling. Sometimes he found it wild, ranting, histrionic, 'a performance' as one of his visitors said; the manner of a charlatan doctor, or a third-rate clown on the London stage. 'It gives me the impression of *how well I read* in the prayers, and *how energetically I preach* in the sermon . . .' (1st July, 1855). Sometimes he found the matter twaddling. Baron Parkes, who was staying for the Assize of 1852, commented upon Andrew's sermon: 'Rubbish might have something good in it — but this sermon was not even rubbish.' Another visitor said, 'I have never heard so great a coxcomb in my life.' Guests whom he brought to church, often seemed uncomfortable.

Sir John himself was fair. He admitted that many parts of many sermons were good, and contained sound teaching. But on the whole he expected the sermon with foreboding. It was a mystery to him that the parish seemed to like it. When Andrew went away, the congregations declined in number. When he came back, they increased again. Strangers came for some miles to hear him. There was something about his concrete way of talking, his definiteness, his emotional sincerity, perhaps even the hardness of his denunciations, which captured the allegiance of the poor. 'It is curious,' wrote Sir John (15th January, 1854), 'that I may almost say every intelligent man who has been here and heard him has been displeased, and most women and weak men like him. Are we who do not approve him "the wise and prudent" who will not listen? It is needful to think of this possibility, and put aside prejudice and pride.'

Sir John was no Calvinist. He disagreed with sermons on predestination, election, the Papists, the millennium, the end of the world, justification by faith only, the uselessness of works for salvation. If he disagreed with Andrew's sermon he would sometimes expound the subject rightly that evening to his family, and sometimes he would choose a counter-sermon to read to them. But two kinds of passages in Andrew's sermons pained him sharply: passages which seemed egotistical, and passages which seemed to point to individuals who could be known.

Andrew held a high doctrine of the ministry. He did not conceal this doctrine from his flock. He told them that he was sent of God to them, that God bestowed His special grace upon His pastors to enable them to guide His people, and therefore it was a dreadful thing in Christian people to withstand the exhortation or rebuke of their pastor. To Sir John's mind, Andrew made it worse by the vanity of his references to himself. Andrew was convinced, *assured*, that he was one of the elect servants of God. It was no merit of his own; God had wrought it when his horse threw him almost through the window of the chemist's shop in Cranbrook. He was never tired, and never shy, of declaring what mighty works God had done through him. Andrew's diary is a series of ejaculations of praise for these works. In the pulpit, these ejaculations sounded like self-praise. Even in the diary they are not always exempt from the sin of self-satisfaction as opposed to the virtue of God-satisfaction. He who is always affirming what marvels have been wrought through his nothingness will find the imp of vanity to be more insidious than he expects. In Andrew the vanity is always harmless. It is never pomposity, never self-centred; when it appears in his diary it does not diminish the affection of the reader. If it was a weakness, it was amiable. But declared from Ketteringham pulpit, these affirmations did not fit Sir John's sense of propriety — the modest behaviour of the true gentleman.

Andrew had learnt that if a sermon was to strike home, it should not be discharged as diffused and undirected shrapnel, but should be aimed at a particular predicament and even a particular person. He would often sit down to write his sermon with a single parishioner in his mind. He would illustrate his points with anecdotes that might strike close: 'As I was coming to church I met a man. . . .' He never mentioned names, but it was not always difficult for the parish to guess who was being thus rebuked. Sir John thought this an invasion of privacy, perhaps running near at times to slander. How shall anyone's character be safe if the clergy denounce him almost by name, from the pulpit?

Andrew, who prayed much about the Boileau household, sometimes directed his arrows at Sir John. The parish penetrated the veil. 'O sir,' said Sir John's old servant Smith to Andrew, probably not without relish, 'how hard you do strike Sir John in your sermons! I really do not know scarcely how to sit sometimes in my seat.' The charge was not always justified. If Andrew preached in general terms of the breaking of the Sabbath, the village supposed him to be preaching against Sir John, whose views upon the keeping of the Sabbath were known to be different. But often the village discerned rightly.

The squire, then, was uncomfortable with his vicar because of the power excited from the pulpit, a power feeble with educated men, explosive with the poor and with some educated women. This power could not be confined to the pulpit. It rippled outwards from the church into the cottages and the stables, the lodges and the gardens. All the housekeepers at the Hall, in succession, came under Andrew's spell. Andrew, despite his personal meekness, had so little fear of saying what he thought, that he was formidable to the parishioners. The nurse at the Hall saw him coming, fled down the street to Smith's lodge, and escaped out of the back of the lodge while he was trying to gain an entry at the front. Sir John's eldest son John, home on holiday from Eton, suddenly vanished when Andrew essayed to speak with him, and was believed to have taken refuge in the hen roost. Andrew thought that these disappearances should probably be attributed to the desire of the fugitives not to be found by Sir John to be talking with the vicar. That may not have been the only reason. Andrew could sometimes be almost overwhelming. He met the Hall gardener, Easton, and told him that he had seen him on a Sunday planning the garden with Sir John. Easton said that his conscience tortured him and he had at once asked forgiveness; but 'my bread depends on my obeying or I must starve'. Andrew said that Moses had left a court and perhaps a kingdom to serve the Lord. Easton sighed, and agreed that such men were happy. Men with consciences or without consciences might for different reasons seek escape if they expected this sort of conversation in the village street.

There was a last reason why Sir John came to distrust, or even to resent, his vicar, and it is the most distasteful reason. He failed to realize how mortally he had wounded Ellen Andrew over the house. She seemed to him harsh, rude, perhaps vulgar. He had once renewed his invitation to dinner, had it refused (though if he had only known it, with an Andrew weakening), and never tried again. It seemed to him impossible to establish the normal relations of society with Andrew's family. Mrs. Andrew, unlike her husband, was not always meek. Andrew submitted when the squire required it. Mrs. Andrew was outspoken, even imperious, by nature.

The following letters speak for themselves — it will be remembered that Sir John sometimes trusted his agents more than was wise:

Ellen Andrew to Sir John Boileau, 13th January, 1845:
Dear Sir John,
Many thanks for your kind intention at various times of supplying our table with game, but I am persuaded that you cannot intend to send such as we have frequently received, indeed the hare sent yesterday was never destroyed by a sportsman, or even snared, but actually died through disease and was a decomposed skeleton; I feel it right to state these things to show that you have

some persons connected with your establishment that are far from trustworthy besides which you know that with our utmost diligence we cannot prevent reports from our own household which must prove injurious to yours; I am sure you will see that you are more concerned in this matter than we can be — the hare received the other week was far too aged to be eaten; besides birds at other times have been thrown away, being in a state of decomposition.

Mr. Andrew and myself feel it our positive duty to inform you of this matter, lest others might be treated in a similar manner, and receive it in a different spirit.

Sir John Boileau to Mrs. Andrew, 14th January, 1845:
Dear Mrs. Andrew,

You and Mr. Andrew only do me justice in believing my wish has always been to find you such game as would be really acceptable and I regret that you should have ever found it otherwise. I have spoken about it so as I trust will infuse caution in future. Let me thank you for the kind feelings towards myself which you express . . . Should any game in future not be such as we could wish, pray send it back with a line to me.

In time Sir John learnt to call these missives *Furores Andrewanae*.

* * * * *

The public behaviour of squire and parson to each other was formal but courteous. Sir John allowed Andrew to walk in Ketteringham park with his family and friends, or to leave his pony in the park stables. Andrew took the greatest care not to forget the Boileau children, writing a congratulatory letter when a son won a prize at Eton, visiting them in sickness, interesting himself in the girls' teaching. When Sir John was ill, Andrew always went to him in bed and there found him at his most gentle. When they could come together and talk on the things of the spirit, their relations seemed on a different plane from their relations when they were engaged in conducting by letter a paper war. Andrew's sternness had a redeeming, self-critical side. 'Saw Sir John shooting with two clergymen Hurnand and Fisher. Did not say "I thank God I am not as other men are" but felt it a mercy I was not.'

He had his allies in Ketteringham Hall itself. Lady Catherine was a quiet shadow, apparently submissive to her powerful husband. But the Hall servants, headed by their housekeeper, seemed to be much upon the side of the vicar. They soon came to church twice on Sunday with regularity, and some of them at least were plainly moved under the vicar's instruction. On 24th February, 1846, his reputation, already considerable, was heightened by an accident. About 8 o'clock that evening, while he was sitting in the study, he heard shouting on the road. He opened the shutters and saw leaping flames. He went out to call his servant Charles, hurried into his hat and shoes and cape, and ran towards the fire. He found that three haystacks at Mr. Buckenham's farm were ablaze; and the flames were threatening to spread to a neighbouring wheatstack only nine feet away, and a barn, full of corn, only six feet away. He found five other men, with two or three buckets between them. Throwing off his hat and coat, and fastening a handkerchief over his nose and mouth, he seized the sheets from the farmhouse, plunged them in water, and with Charles' help threw them over the unburning wheatstack. Soon a little crowd of some twenty men had collected, and Andrew found that they looked to him for leadership. Dripping with sweat, he organized them in a double line to pass buckets, kettles, tubs, and any other vessel that would hold water. For a few minutes he was almost overcome by the smoke and forced to retreat for a rest; soon afterwards he took a turn at working the pump. They left the haystacks to burn, but by half-past ten had averted all danger to wheatstack or barn. Andrew put on his hat and coat, spoke a word of consolation to the distressed farmer's wife and her children and hurried home. Ellen stripped him and washed him, made him sit with his legs in a hot bath, poured chocolate copiously into him, and put him into a hot bed. He was amused when he heard that Hethersett villagers, seeing his muscular arms throwing water, had said, 'Is that the slim delicate parson at Ketteringham?' The imp of vanity was dancing behind his ear. He could not resist a twinge of self-satisfaction at his gallantry. 'It was the remark of John Newton,' he reminded himself; ' "if a Christian is but a shoeblack he should be the best in the parish".'

It was clear that everything was leading towards a breach between squire and parson — the game, the vestry, the schoolmistress, the factions in the parish, the laughter in church. It was only a matter of time before the running argument crossed the border into conflict. It came in October, 1846; and it is interesting that the battle should have begun in a way typical of the history of Calvinist churches — an attempt by the ecclesiastical authority to excommunicate a citizen against the wish of the secular authority.

Andrew declined to christen Barnard's children because the Barnards had chosen Mrs. George Daniels as godmother. The refusal had been public. For Andrew was accustomed to baptize babies in the middle of evening prayer, and the Barnards had brought their boys to the service. Andrew had come down the aisle to the font and, seeing how things were, had returned to the reading-desk. He had established a rule that all godparents must be communicants. Mrs. Daniels was not a communicant. But the case had this peculiarity, that she wished to be a communicant, and had been forbidden by the vicar to attend the Sacrament. 'He is trying to carry the church with a high hand,' said Sir John.

On 8th October, Andrew attended a lecture which the squire, always anxious for the wider education of the village, had arranged in Ketteringham Hall on 'The Structure of Plants' by the Reverend Mr. Sidney. Andrew was unimpressed by Mr. Sidney, doubtless wondering whether such a subject was suitable, and religious enough, for a minister of Christ. After the lecture he drew the squire aside and said that he thought Mrs. Daniels had better not come to the Lord's Supper. He did not receive a direct negative, but he judged from the squire's attitude that he would urge her to come. Five days later he received a letter in which Sir John told him that he had laid the case of Mrs. Daniels before the bishop of Norwich.

Andrew was indignant. 'What a weak man! What has the bishop to do about judging the fitness of one of my people to attend the Lord's Supper? Well does the Apostle say "As much as in you lieth live peaceably etc." ' Later in the day he received a letter from the bishop summoning him to Norwich to discuss the case of Mrs. Daniels.

Andrew was now roused. On a rainy 14th October, he wrote a note to Sir John asking for an interview. He was told to come at 7 p.m.

Leaving Ellen and the governess, Miss Rising, engaged at

prayer for him, he entered the Hall in trepidation, expecting rough treatment, and was shown by the servant into the study. The door from the dining-room opened and he was kindly and courteously drawn to the table, where the whole Boileau family was eating dessert. In the presence of the family Sir John congratulated him upon the beauty of his house and garden, and Andrew was pleased. The two men then retired to the study.

Andrew put the bishop's summons into his hand, and asked, 'What do you think my feelings must be at being thus summoned by my squire before the bishop?'

Sir John read the bishop's letter and said that he was surprised at some of the expressions in it. But after a few words he added, 'Well, it is all well, we shall have it all out now.' His quick temper began to rise to the surface. Andrew said, 'I have done all in my power to live happily with you.' Sir John lifted up his fist and for three hours poured recriminations upon Andrew's head. 'From the first hour of my coming to Ketteringham to the present time you have pursued a course of insult towards me. I first saw you near Hethel when you insultingly refused my kind invitation to dinner.'

'I refused,' said Andrew, 'only lest I should give offence to others who had invited me. You mistake. The first time I saw you was when I called at this house and you did not even ask me to sit down.'

'Oh, I see! then it was your malicious evil spirit that led you afterwards to act so towards me. . . . When you did once dine with me, Mrs. Andrew was invited and did not even condescend to send an excuse to Lady Catherine — and when you, sir, were leaving that night you tossed your head in a dignified manner and said, "I came today merely in honour to the bishop." '

He attacked the frank notes which Ellen, in her zeal, was in the habit of sending. 'She has constantly insulted all my family and has said to the poor "Miss Boileau is no lady." '

Andrew denied it. They argued over little Sarah Cooper and her removal from the school. The recrimination mounted into a volley. 'You, sir, who are too sanctified to give attention to temporal matters and can't be spoken to on a Sabbath about earthly things, you make yourself a complete pope. You set yourself as an idol and will make all worship you: you know it is so. The pride of your heart is enormous, your pride of heart you have no idea of.

'But I give you to understand — I will rule this parish and the minister shall be subservient to me. Then you try to force the people to come to church twice a day. Then the church is crowded with people from other parishes; and you require sponsors to be communicants — which I will resist to the utmost as long as ever I am in this parish. Then my daughters are not to have what children they please in the Sunday School, but they shall. And I will turn every family out of the parish who dares to disobey me.

'I find no hope of our peace, and therefore I will lay everything before the bishop, and Mrs. Andrew's insulting letters are all tied up there ready. And tomorrow, . . . before the bishop, sir, you will answer for yourself.'

Andrew tried vainly to calm him down. So he advanced, seized the squire's hand, shook it, bade him goodnight, and hurried home. He did not regain Wood Hall until after midnight, and then sat up to tell Ellen all that had passed. He told her humorously that his two texts for sermons next Sunday should be, 'A night much to be remembered', and 'Who can tell what shall be on the morrow?'

The morrow came, 15th October, 1846, and, 'full of divine peace', Andrew set out for Norwich. He called upon his friend Gladstone and asked his prayers, then upon his friend Perowne to do the same. Perowne advised him to demand from the bishop a written text of Sir John's complaints, and to reserve his defence until he could plead in the presence of two clergymen. He reached the palace, and was shown up, through its long rambling passages, into the bishop's room. The bishop, to his surprise, took him warmly by the hand, inquired particularly of Mrs. Andrew and the children, refused to let him sit upon a chair but drew him to the sofa, and was solicitous that he should not sit near an open window.

'Now, Mr. Andrew,' said the bishop, 'will you just tell me about this matter?'

Andrew made a long statement. The bishop wrote it all down in long hand, covering nearly four quarto pages, and the writing took nearly an hour. Then the bishop took other papers, and perused Sir John's complaints. He said, 'Well, Mr. Andrew, I see you have told me all. It exactly accords with Sir John's letter.'

'I am glad to find it does, my Lord.' He found that he was chiefly accused of refusing Mrs. Daniels as godmother to Barnard's children. Anxious to show that this was not due to any ill-feeling towards Mrs. Daniels, he said, 'It was only a few months ago, the woman, being ill, manifested an earnest desire for me to be with her, and from that time she has shown the most kindly feeling. And to show also that I am not scrupulous about my communicants, my Lord, I found five when I came to Ketteringham and we now number sixty, and forty were in attendance last time.'

The bishop looked surprised and pleased. He said, 'You must not keep the woman away from the Table on account of her character, but if she has the itch you should strongly recommend her not to come.' He turned to make peace. 'Sir John,' he said, 'is a most valuable man and does an immensity of good. I hope you will yield to him in everything you can.'

'Indeed I will,' said Andrew.

'I was once the rector where my brother was the squire, and there it was hard work, but I yielded wherever I could conscientiously.'

'My Lord,' replied Andrew, 'Sir John misunderstands me, and we do not see things alike. For instance, though I am sure I would not say anything against him, it is with grief I speak it and I have prayed to God for him. But some time since he asked me to go round the parish with him and hold spiritual conversation, to show the poor we are united. Now my Lord, when the family come to church in the morning and, as I have been told, play at games in the afternoon — I am sure, my Lord, you will see it would have a very bad effect upon my people if we were to appear to be united in spiritual matters.'

The bishop was silent.

Andrew felt that the bishop had throughout behaved 'nobly, kindly and Christianly'. He wondered where his accuser was. He was sure that Sir John was somewhere in the palace. He fancied sometimes that he might be hiding behind the wainscot. (Sir John had gone over to see Burgh Castle.) 'I feel as a captain, who, having anticipated a glorious victory over an enemy, discovers he had stolen away during the night. . . . The coward never showed himself. I hope shame kept him away. Well, I will pray for him, hoping he is not "past feeling".'

Three days later, at the Sunday morning service, he found large congregations waiting. He expected that the Boileaus would not be among them and probably that Sir John would forbid the servants to come. But they were all there except the housekeeper, who came to the afternoon service. As he came into the churchyard, the eldest Miss Boileau (Ama) was advancing from the opposite gate. He hesitated. If he went up to her, would she spurn him? Summoning up great cheerfulness, he hastened to catch her; and she received him and shook his hand as usual. Her Bible dropped in the mud, and Andrew picked it up and told her that he would take it into the vestry and have it cleaned. He thought the little accident providential. He did not meet Sir John himself until the service on Christmas Day, when he came into the vestry to inquire after Ellen, who had just given birth to another baby. But he had sent to the vicarage a brace of hares only three weeks after the bishop's summons. And Andrew, at the bishop's request, had admitted Mrs. Daniels to the Sacrament and baptized Barnard's children.[1]

Sir John had conquered. In 1844, he was still trying to secure the office of churchwarden for himself and Andrew was still trying to prevent it. By 1847, Sir John had captured the office. In 1844, the vicar had retained his rights over the shooting on his glebe, which adjoined Ketteringham park. By the next year he was forced to allow the squire to secure the shooting rights, and could only maintain a feeble independence by insisting on a fixed agreement.

In 1850, Sir John removed the church registers from the vicar's care ('My nature,' said Andrew, 'says, Tell the bishop. Grace says, As much as in you lieth live peaceably with all men'), locked them in an iron chest provided by himself (doubtless the chest still to be found in the vestry at Ketteringham), and kept the keys. Whenever he was present, he presided over the meetings of the parish vestry. Whenever he was not present, the other churchwarden, his bailiff and henchman

[1] The register shows that the Barnard boys were baptized on 1st November.

Mr. Blomfield, presided. He removed the gates from the church-yard, to close them against strangers, and on the Sunday before the gates were closed stationed his gardener to prevent strangers from driving carriages into the churchyard. He demanded that Andrew should refrain from leaving his pony in the churchyard during service, told him that it desecrated the place, and that the village might suppose the squire to be refusing room in the stable and so to be on bad terms with his parson. Poor Sarah Cooper, who had fallen in love with a young man named Chubb but had been forced to break the connexion because Chubb was caught poaching the squire's game, had already been removed from her post as schoolmistress.[1]

The policy of submission was now established. It had behind it not only reason, prudence and Christian peaceableness, but the authority of the bishop. It seemed a small thing that Miss Beasley, Sarah Cooper's successor as schoolmistress, refused to accept Sir John's invitation to the village dance in the New Year of 1853.

[1] Sarah Cooper died of consumption, aged thirty-two, and was buried in the churchyard. Her interesting inscription, by Sharpe of Cromer, has been worn away and is now illegible on the stone. But it may be read in a burials book, with copies of the epitaphs, kept in the vestry.

VI

JAMES RUSH

JOHN ELLIOTT BOILEAU's twenty-first birthday fell upon 28th September, 1848. He had been educated at Eton and was now at University College, Oxford. His presents were sent to his room after family prayers: from his father a Purdey's best new double-barrelled gun, costing £52. 10s. 0d., and from his mother a pretty table clock. During breakfast the Hethersett band played, and the bells of Ketteringham church were rung. After an early lunch they went out to Lady Catherine's pit in the grounds and planted an elm tree, about sixteen feet high, at the south-west corner; beneath the elm was placed a tin containing a sixpenny piece from each of the party staying in the house, and Sir John made a little speech which was cheered. At five o'clock dinner, Sir John sent round two from the last three bottles of his famous old sherry of the year 1796 and proposed the heir's health. The garden terrace and the pleasure grounds were illuminated with coloured lamps and coloured paper lanterns, one of the effects being John's initials and the date. Bishop Stanley and his family came to promenade in the grounds. The gates of the park were thrown open to the villagers and, on the opposite side of the lake, the proprietor and pyro-technist of the Vauxhall Gardens, Norwich, who had arranged the illuminations, directed a grand display of fireworks.

On the following day the tenants came to dinner. Some thirty-four sat down in the great hall (one farmer, William Howes, with whom the squire was not on good terms, failing to appear). While the ladies looked down from the gallery, Sir John made a speech but was discontented with it. He would have liked to have praised the virtues of his heir; but as he had just been engaged in paying off various debts contracted at Oxford and reluctantly admitted, he felt sadly confined in what he could say. It was a lame speech, he thought; and then he tried to compensate by proposing the Queen's health in an unusually long speech, but felt that this too was a failure and was made nervous because Huntley, the butler, had failed to charge some of the glasses. He was more satisfied with the rest of his efforts, and was pleased that, though he observed a tendency of *uproariousness* in Mr. Read being damped by his neighbours, only one of the tenants was drunk — Baker of Forncett — 'which as he is a discredit to the estate and must go is as well'. The gentry left the dinner at quarter-past nine, but Read and a few others stayed to consume four more bottles of wine and, Sir John was told, made a very feeling and complimentary speech about him. Then there was dancing, and he felt warmed and grateful towards the servants, thinking to himself that they were more like friends than hired attendants. The kitchen maid, Elizabeth Moore, was taken with hysterics, believed to be caused by over-fatigue.

He was not without qualms of conscience. On the following Monday, when there was a great ball for the county, kept up with spirit till four o'clock, he feared that the musicians went away drunk. If the musicians went away drunk, he feared that the festivities were sinful and ought not to be allowed, even for the sake of his family. On Tuesday the whole party went over to Tacolneston where the Hall and grounds were decorated with flags and mottoes and garlands. They walked in procession up the avenue to the Hall, accompanied by a band, with guns firing, and the church bells ringing.

In front of the Hall, on either side of the central grass plot, were two long tables, loaded with plum pudding, roast beef and vegetables. At one of the tables sat a hundred men, at the other a hundred women — the cottagers and labourers of the parish. It made Sir John's heart come into his mouth to see their cordiality. After dinner Sir John stood upon a table and proposed John's health with three times three, and got Howes to lead the cheering. Mr. Corbould, the rector of Tacolneston, proposed Sir John's health with much emotion, and Sir John returned thanks, and told all the poor that if they wanted a friend they were to rely on Lady Catherine and himself and come over to them at Ketteringham. After 'God save the Queen', Mr. Corbould proposed Lady Catherine's health; the squire led her forward saying, as she could not speak herself, that she felt a deep interest in the people and thanked them all. They were cheered down the avenue as they drove away, and at the gate, guarded by a policeman, found about a hundred of the neighbouring people who had not been invited to partake. He threw amongst them from side to side all the silver he had collected at the Hall before coming away. At the church they stopped to listen to the bells ringing, John got down to speak to the ringers, and Sir John sent them a sovereign.

The next day, Wednesday, Sir John brought out from Norwich a fiddler and his boy with an octave flute, to play for the servants' dance in Ketteringham Hall that evening. Sir John and Lady Catherine opened the dancing, the whole family joined ('except the governess, who seems from nervous ill-health to be foolish about it'), and about midnight the squire proposed John's health and thanked the servants for their zeal, good temper, and exertions. The servants chaired John round the room, and then danced until two o'clock. Huntley assured Sir John next morning that there had been no excessive drunkenness or misbehaviour.

On Thursday the children's games were held. Sir John found that Easton the gardener's preparations were behind, and himself set to work with hammer and nails, putting up banners, archways, goal-posts. The people assembled at Cannell's lodge; and at the sound of the dinner gong, a procession advanced to the Hall, led by Ringer, the gamekeeper, and the Hethersett band. At the iron gate the squire and John stopped them and told them that they were going to have old English games for an hour. They climbed a soapy mast for a shoulder of mutton, ran in sacks, attempted a long jump and raced blindfold with wheel-barrows, and finally a good foot race in which the coachman and the footman ran, and the footman could have beaten all but preferred to give way and let others get the prizes.

Mr. Andrew arrived as the games were ending. At the sound of the gong the people paraded again and, headed by the band, moved into the Hall, 121 of them. Andrew made to go away, but Sir John called him into the Hall, asked the crowd to stand up, and called upon him to say grace. As the people fell to their roast beef and plum pudding, Andrew turned to Sir John and said, 'I enjoy the sight and think well of it. I wish you and your family well.' Sir John took Lady Catherine up into the gallery and surveyed the scene with pleasure. He called upon Mr. Bickmore to say the closing grace, and then proposed John's health. His speech was something to this effect: I and my family have not resided here long, and have not yet gained your hereditary affection. But I hope that you have found Lady Catherine and me your friends. I have had to do some things to punish the wrong, and make examples; but this was only for the happiness of all, as without mutual good conduct and respect the parish cannot be happy. But we have rejoiced whenever we have found any opportunity of showing kindness. This is our real delight; and we are sure John will do the same, and we hope that he will have the hereditary attachment from the children of those present — and has now their own respect and love, and will so drink health and happiness to him. That was the substance of Sir John's speech; and after John had thanked them for the toast, they sang 'God save the Queen'.

It was the end of the festivities, which, as the squire hoped, would be long remembered.

John was never to succeed to the title, nor to the ownership of Ketteringham Hall, nor to the hereditary attachment of the people. He was called to the Bar, and became for two terms private secretary to Lord John Russell. When Russell retired from office, he went out to the Crimean campaign, as it ended, and caught a fever on the Danube, from which he never recovered. He was sent for his health to the Mediterranean, but died at Dieppe on 8th October, 1861.

*   *   *   *   *

Between Ketteringham and Wymondham lay in solitary, pseudo-Tudor splendour the house called Stanfield Hall, surrounded by a moat and then by its park. Its owner since 1837 was a distinguished lawyer, Isaac Jermy, the Recorder of Norwich. Though Stanfield Hall lay within the parish of Wymondham, Mr. Jermy sometimes attended Ketteringham church to sit at the feet of Andrew. With him lived his son by a first wife, oddly called Isaac Jermy Jermy, and his son's wife and one grand-daughter.

The possession of Stanfield Hall was the subject of a vexatious lawsuit. Mr. Jermy's real name was Preston; he had taken the name Jermy when he succeeded to the Jermy estate. There were distant members of the Jermy family who contended that the Prestons had no right to Stanfield Hall. About 11 a.m. on

24th September, 1838 (Andrew was probably away on his annual holiday at Gorleston), one of the claimants, Mr. Larner, appeared at Stanfield Hall with a band of eighty men, cheering and waving their hats, in which most of them were wearing laurel leaves. When the housekeeper barred the kitchen door, Larner broke it open with a crowbar. His men carried the only two servants in residence out of the house, cleared out the furniture, and barricaded the windows, apparently against a siege. Mr. Jermy, who seemed to have had warning or had disappeared at the approach of the marauders, arrived from Wymondham with two police constables who could do little but protect the furniture, now exposed in the yard to pouring rain. Mr. Jermy, who was a magistrate, read the Riot Act outside his own front door and then outside the back door, and warned the invaders that they would be guilty of felony if they remained an hour after the Act was read. One of the constables was injured with a bludgeon when he got hold of an invader and was set upon by a rescue party. About 5.45 p.m. a detachment of the 4th Dragoon Guards arrived from Norwich, surrounded the Hall, and ostentatiously loaded their weapons. The invaders were given five minutes to surrender. At the Lent Assizes of 1839, they were given short terms of imprisonment, even Larner escaping with three months in gaol.

On the fringe of the Stanfield Hall estate lay Potash Farm, occupied by a family named Rush. The affairs of Mr. Jermy were much entangled with those of James Rush the farmer; and between 1846 and 1848 their relations were carried into a court of law. Rush, an ignorant man, had convinced himself that Jermy was the wrongful owner of Stanfield Hall and supported Larner and the family claimants.

At the end of October, 1844, Rush's father died from the accidental firing of a gun in his own kitchen. Andrew visited the house (though it was not in his parish) and found James Rush very suspicious of any attempt to minister consolation. During the next few months Andrew was delighted to find Rush paying more heed to the ministrations in Ketteringham church. He would always sit in a particular pew, he came faithfully to receive the Sacrament, and was sometimes observed to be weeping like a child as he partook, his feelings evidently and deeply moved. Andrew received much comfort during 1845 from the worship of Mr. Rush and his family. He seemed an affectionate husband, and Andrew was impressed with the piety of Mrs. Rush. He could not quite make out Rush himself. There was a strangeness about him, a reserve, a liability to fits of depression. The village did not like him. In the cottages it was widely gossiped that the death of his father had not been accidental, and the villagers thought of him as a kind of ogre. Andrew observed all this, and yet hoped that here would be found a sign of the workings of grace. Seeing the man's unpopularity, he dreamed a strange dream. Mr. Rush was at the vicarage when the house was surrounded by a crowd of armed men wanting to murder him. Andrew dreamed that he knelt down and prayed for the preservation of Rush, ordered the shutters to be closed and then took him upstairs to hide him from the mob, first in a chest and then behind the battlements above the dining-room window. He awoke from the dream really frightened.

On 22nd November, 1845, Mrs. Rush died, and something seemed to go wrong with her husband's piety. He started absenting himself irregularly from church, and Andrew noted that he was not in a satisfactory state. The village began to gossip that the relations between Rush and his young governess were not what they should be. He needed a housekeeper, and Andrew exerted himself to find a pious woman, writing to the Readers Society on his behalf. He found it curiously difficult to recommend the man's character warmly. Rush pleaded, for his absence from church, that he went to Wymondham to avoid the Ketteringham gossip about himself and his governess. The housekeeper arrived and appeared to be sedate enough.

In December, 1846, Rush changed his governess. A new girl arrived, by name Emily Sandford. He brought her to church, but she seemed to the vicar a young lady perfectly indifferent to divine things. A month later the housekeeper left the premises. She had found that Mr. Rush was not, after all, respectable. The gossip of the village had been justified. He continued, however, irregularly to attend Ketteringham church. Andrew sometimes directed parts of his sermon at him. He prayed passionately on his behalf, as he prayed for others erring among his flock.

On the evening of Tuesday, 28th October, 1848, Mr.

Jermy of Stanfield Hall finished his dinner soon after 8 p.m., left his son and daughter-in-law to drink tea and play picquet in the drawing-room, and wandered out of the front door into the porch. As he came out, a man with something black round his head stepped out of the night, put a pistol to Mr. Jermy's heart, and shot him dead.

The younger Jermy, at cards in the drawing-room, heard the shot. He went through the hall, there met the intruder, who had come into the house through the side door, and was shot down in the hall. The young Mrs. Jermy came running out of the drawing-room and found only the dead body of her husband in the hall. She began screaming for help; one of the maids, Eliza Chastney, ran out of the servant's hall and grasped her screaming mistress by the waist, crying, 'My dear mistress, what's the matter?' At this moment the gunman stepped out of the dining-room, fired twice at the women, ran through the side door and escaped into the night. Eliza was hit in the leg and Mrs. Jermy in the arm, but neither was killed. After a suitable interval, the butler emerged from the pantry where he had been hiding, and ran out of the house to a neighbouring farmer for help. The cook seized the girl of fourteen and took refuge with her in the coach-house. A few hundred yards away a party of servants heard the shots and carried the news to Wymondham. A telegraph went to Norwich, and by 2 a.m. a strong detachment of the Norwich police was at Stanfield Hall. They went immediately to Potash Farm, a mile away, surrounded it, and at dawn arrested James Rush. Sir John Boileau came down to breakfast that morning and was told by Huntley, the butler, that Rush had murdered Mr. Jermy (and then, so Huntley had heard, shot himself).

Sir John spent the day of 2nd November with other magistrates at Wymondham Bridewell, examining Rush and his governess (or mistress) Emily Sandford. Emily Sandford had at first declared that Rush was out that night for a few minutes only; but in this statement she declared that she had been telling a lie and that he had been out for far longer. Rush looked across at her as she went out and said, 'You have said all you can to hang me.'

*   *   *   *   *

Into the celebrated trial of Rush this history need not enter. Sir John Boileau was one of the examining magistrates and was present throughout the trial. The butler and the maid, Eliza Chastney, claimed to have recognized his build, though not his face, which was disguised. His mistress, Emily Sandford, gave evidence that he had been out of Potash Farm for approximately the right length of time. He had been heard to utter threats against Mr. Jermy. The gunman had dropped paper inside Stanfield Hall, paper of a variety sold by Jarrolds of Norwich, and paper of the same variety from Jarrolds was found in Potash Farm. Rush, in his folly and obstinacy, refused legal aid and conducted his own defence. He conducted it so boorishly and ignorantly as to prejudice the entire court against him. The case was in effect undefended; Baron Rolfe directed the jury to find the prisoner guilty. Sir John was entirely convinced of the guilt. No one told the judge and jury that local prejudice against Rush was already so widespread that the identification by the servants of a disguised man must be regarded as doubtful. No defending lawyer pointed out that Emily Sandford in her first statement had described him as out for a few minutes only, and that her later and damning statements appeared to be marked by a measure of animus against the prisoner; that she had given Sir John Boileau and others an impression of being altogether untrustworthy, of being ready to swear to anything, and yet that her evidence was so vital to the conviction that they had even considered holding her on a charge of forgery to prevent her running away. No one asked the jury whether it was credible that a man, notorious for having uttered threats against Mr. Jermy, should have entered Mr. Jermy's house where everyone knew him well, killed two men, and returned quietly to his farmhouse next door to await the inevitable arrest and feign surprise when it came — and, if it was credible, was it not the duty of the jury to bring in a verdict of insanity? None of these things was said to judge and to jury; and so on 4th April, 1849, Rush was sentenced to be hanged by the neck until he was dead. Sir John looked down from the gallery upon the crowded court-room, put his head in his hands, and prayed in quietness for the condemned man.

Andrew had endeavoured to see Rush before the trial, but had been refused permission. He did not dare to go to the

Assize lest he should be called by Rush to give evidence of his
character. Like everyone else, he believed absolutely in Rush's
guilt. But he heard that Rush had been taken back to Norwich
Castle still protesting his innocence. The governor of the Castle
told him that he had never met anyone like Rush, anyone so
obstinate and dogged, and that Rush had refused to allow the
chaplain of the gaol, Mr. Brown, to read or pray with him. But
within a few days, on 9th April, a message came to Andrew that
Rush wished to see him. He hurried to the cell.

Rush was standing near the door of his cell and gazed at
Andrew impassively. Andrew seized his hand, turned his head
away and wept, but uttered no word. Rush began to tremble,
and then a wave of emotion and grief swept over him and he
sank down on his bed. Andrew kept the silence a few minutes
longer. Then he said, 'My poor friend, how little could I have
expected to see you here.' Rush said nothing but went on
weeping. They sat together for nearly two hours, saying very
little to each other, Andrew reading occasional texts from the
Bible. Three days later, he came again, in the unwelcome
company of Mr. Brown, the prison chaplain. This time Rush
distressed Andrew by protesting his innocence.

'O sir, I am quite innocent, and it would break my heart if
you did not think so.'

'I would not be uncharitable,' said Andrew, 'but place yourself in my situation. How could I with all the evidence think
so?'

He was puzzled, perturbed, by Rush. The man had been
proved in court to be a monster, and yet apart from this absurd
protestation of innocence, he seemed to have a soft and penitent
heart — if a monster, then a weeping monster. At a visit two
days later, Rush shocked him by claiming to be in a state of
grace. 'How often,' asked Andrew grimly, 'have you knelt by
the side of Emily Sandford and said "Lead us not into temptation", and then committed fornication?'

He had begun to lose hope of bringing Rush to confession
before the last. He thought something might have been done if
he had only been allowed to see Rush alone, without the company of Mr. Brown, the chaplain. But it was not permitted, and
on Saturday, 20th April (after the rejection of a petition from
the citizens of Norwich that the execution be postponed till

Monday so that the Saturday market might not be disturbed), the end came.

On the day of execution Rush attended chapel at ten o'clock with the other prisoners. Andrew had arranged with the governor that he also might attend the service and sat in the governor's pew. He watched, indeed he hoped, for any sign of weakening in the firm exterior, but Rush answered the responses clearly from his iron-paled pew between two warders, and his hand was not shaking. Andrew asked if he might speak with him after the service, and he was brought to the reading-desk. Andrew with tears in his eyes urged him to confess. Rush laid his hands upon the rails, looked upwards and called God to witness his innocence. Andrew's heart was so moved that he could hardly speak; he bid Rush 'adieu for ever', retired to the magistrates' room and sank almost fainting into a chair. In a few minutes Rush was brought into the room to be pinioned by Calcraft, the public executioner. As Calcraft fastened the ropes, with Andrew weeping quietly in a corner, Rush, who was still perfectly cool, said with a shrug, 'This don't go easy; I don't want the rope to hurt me.' It was moved to give him relief; and the procession formed to march out to the public scaffold, erected upon the bridge over the Castle moat. Aloft, above the scaffold, an immense black flag waved in the breeze. The windows, the housetops and even the roof of the church tower, were crowded with spectators. The trains from Yarmouth and elsewhere had been coming in full of passengers, and some twelve or thirteen thousand of the citizens of Norfolk, including a fair number of women and children, witnessed the death of Rush, as the knell tolled from the tower of St. Peter Mancroft. He never faltered.

Andrew was not among the spectators. As a little child he had been taken to see the public execution of five men of Northampton who had robbed his uncle, and had been carried almost fainting out of the crowd. He walked as far as the gateway behind Rush, was pleased to see him look round at him once. But the moment he saw the rope fixed he turned and hurried back into the Castle, and in a few minutes Calcraft, the executioner, came in saying, 'All is over.'

*   *   *   *   *

On the morrow Andrew was surprised to find a larger congregation than usual at the morning service in Ketteringham church. The interest aroused throughout Norfolk by the Stanfield Hall murders had been universal. Every detail had been reported at length in the press, and the visits of Andrew had not escaped the reporters. Andrew awoke to find himself a famous man. He suspected that these fresh strangers at his church had come with the hope of hearing something about Rush. In the afternoon he found the same. So he said to the congregation, 'If spared till next Lord's Day, I will give a little sketch of my interviews in the cell, though I wish that I could altogether forget the circumstance, for my health is impaired.'

A week later, on Sunday, 28th April, 1849, he went to morning service as usual and was surprised to find an immense congregation. 'You are mistaken,' he said. 'I intend to speak of Rush in the afternoon.' Some of them said, 'We are come to secure seats for the afternoon.' By one o'clock there was quite a crowd in the churchyard and the church was so crowded that Ellen could hardly descend from the gallery. Between services Andrew went through the gate into Ketteringham park and walked in Sir John's plantation.

When he came back, there was an unforgettable scene. Inside the church the people were stuffed like figs in a cask. Outside the church there was a large crowd in the churchyard. Some of them begged him to preach in the open air so that all might hear. Andrew considered it. Though he knew that Sir John had gone away, he knew that he would have disapproved. If the squire disapproved of him preaching to a small number of strangers inside his church, he would vehemently disapprove of him preaching to a large number of strangers outside his church. He remembered the policy of submission, and decided to preach inside the church. It seemed however, to be impossible to get inside the church to preach.

Luckily Mr. Parnell, the curate, had succeeded in pushing his way through to the reading-desk. Andrew left him to conduct the service and himself retired to Sir John's study where once reproaches had been heaped upon his head for more than three hours. Copeman, the clerk, was instructed to fetch him when they were singing the last hymn. Copeman found him kneeling at his prayers in the study when he came running to say that it was time.

He struggled through to the pulpit, gloomily and with a throbbing heart. A lady quite unknown to him amused him by using him as a means of getting nearer to the pulpit, clutching him and saying, 'May I lay hold of you?' He dragged her with him through the press to the reading-desk, where he remembered that he had forgotten to put on his gown. As he stood in the pulpit it seemed to him that the people were piled on top of each other; the windows of the church were darkened by the faces trying to peer through them. Sir John's pew, which was locked, had been scaled by about fifty people. He was determined that he would be heard outside if possible, so he turned away from the large Boileau inscription on the gallery and directed his voice across the aisle to the little lancet window, which was open, and spoke at the stretch of his voice, probably too loudly for some of the multitude in the little church. It was afterwards calculated that about two thousand people had squeezed themselves into church and churchyard.

It was a strange sermon. He had chosen only a text and had left the matter of the sermon to take care of itself. The text was Hosea iv. 17, 'Ephraim is joined to idols: let him alone.' As the matter was extempore he altogether deceived himself about the time which he was occupying and, when at the end he consulted Ellen's watch, he found that he had preached for two hours and twenty minutes.

Why had Rush not confessed his crime in penitence? Because his heart had been so hardened that God left him in his sins and bestowed not upon him the grace of penitence. He had hardened his own heart by a course of sensuality and of covetousness. He had forged and lied and stolen — and yet (Andrew's sense of forgiveness kept breaking in) he had used generously the money which he gained. Many would remember his gifts with gratitude. He set himself upon a course to lechery and to fraud in spite of his education, his opportunity to become a useful member of society, his clear views of divine truth in late years. For 'not only had he a liberal education, but he sat under a gospel ministry. I am not afraid or ashamed to declare this; for were I to say otherwise, I should deny that sovereign grace which God has bestowed on his servant. . . . He was for several years accustomed to sit in a pew exactly opposite to me; and it is remarkable that, whatever might be the weather, when many who lived within a few yards of this house of God were ready to make any trifling circumstance an excuse for their absence, we seldom found his pew empty' — though he had ceased attending the church at all more than twelve months before the murder, about the time when Emily Sandford came to live with him. Andrew described what had happened in the condemned cell. He did not believe that Rush's weeping in church, or his quest for truth in his cell, were pretended. The world (like Sir John Boileau, though Andrew did not mention the squire's name from the pulpit) believed that Rush was a hypocrite, that these religious impressions were artificial. 'I do not believe it was so. Whilst I have been preaching I have many times seen him weeping as if his heart would break; and you, my people, have often witnessed the same thing, heard his sobs, and expressed your pity for him. Would a man weep thus in hypocrisy, and that too in the midst of a congregation, and surrounded by his young family? Would a man sob in hypocrisy? No! It was God's word bruising the conscience, but not breaking the heart — the Spirit enlightening the understanding, but not influencing the will and the affections — the remorse for having done wrong, but not a Saviour's love constraining to what was right.'

And so the evil spirit was suffered to destroy him, as once the evil spirits were suffered to go into the Gadarene swine. When the Lord gives a sinner up, the devil takes possession of him, and the wicked is driven away in his wickedness till he comes to the bottomless pit. That poor man, on his way to the scaffold, had his arms bounds with cords, so that it was impossible for him to escape; but these cords were only an emblem of the manner in which he was holden by the cords of his sins. This miserable man believed a delusion — before his condemnation he believed constantly that he would be acquitted at his trial. He succeeded in persuading his family to believe it likewise, so that they even made preparations for his return home; he wrote more than one letter to the Queen, requesting her personally to investigate the accusations of his accusers. Satan was allowed thus to delude him with vain hopes and useless endeavours for the purpose of keeping him calm and quiet in his sin. He deluded himself with the idea that he was generally regarded as innocent. 'I had no doubt of his guilt, and I told him so.'

Some people are ready to say that public executions are not only disgraceful, but unbecoming a Christian nation. They are trying to repeal the law of capital punishment, even for murder. 'I am sure of this, that were it not for one thing, I should be among the first to lift up my voice against them. I think they do a great deal of harm, that they may harden many in sin, and brutalize the mind; but there is one thing which keeps me from daring for a moment to say that they are wrong, and that is the word of God. It is written, "Whoso sheddeth man's blood, by man shall his blood be shed".'

He died a sinner and impenitent. And yet men have attached to him the vilest names. 'My spirit had often been pained by salutation of this kind — "Have you seen that foul hypocrite?", "What do you think of that wretch?", "Is he not a devil incarnate?". Such language does not surprise me for two reasons — men do not consider that all his black deeds were caused by one thing, *a bad heart*, and that their own natural heart was no better than his. What a thought! Your heart or mine, left to itself, is ready for any of the crimes laid to this man. Men generally dislike this doctrine; and well they may. He who alone searches the heart, and tries the reins, has written with His own finger, "The heart is desperately wicked".'

And so Andrew led on that mighty congregation towards penitence, and the faith that their redemption rested upon the free grace of Christ; and thence to beware the world and its temptation — the ballroom, the theatre, the masquerade, the infidel book, the Sunday newspaper. Let them search themselves to discover whether the world was not leading them down the same Gadarene slope. And if they were different from Rush, 'consider who made us to differ? Whence comes our change? Did it begin with ourselves? It was grace; the sovereign grace of a Triune Jehovah.'

> Grace first inscribed my name
>   In God's eternal book.
> 'Twas grace that led me to the Lamb
>   Who all my sorrows took.

The crowd seemed in no hurry to disperse. They drifted

slowly away. In the evening the servant Charles came to the window of the vicarage to say that reporters had been in the church.

The overstrain at last caught him again, and next day forced him away from Ketteringham in the hope that he might forget the last few weeks. At the hotel that night he was astonished to find on the table a newspaper with a report of his sermon occupying nearly two columns; and accompanying it a letter asking leave to publish the whole. He was confounded, and went to Dr. Marsh, who was also staying in the hotel, to ask his advice.

'You must publish this,' exclaimed Marsh.

'Impossible,' said Andrew, 'for I have not even a sketch. The whole was extempore.'

'Then you must revise the publisher's notes.'

He laboured to reduce his two hours and twenty minutes to a sermon of three-quarters of an hour, and perhaps cut a half or two-thirds of what the shorthand writer reported him to have said. The sermon was published on 1st June. It sold in great numbers.

* * * * *

The publication of the sermon on Rush was not good for Andrew's soul. He found himself famous overnight. Hitherto his vision had been limited to Ketteringham and Hethel and Hethersett, to the needs of his simple flock and the occasional meetings in the city of Norwich. Now he found himself in demand as a preacher; he was engaged to conduct missions; he began to hobnob upon equal terms with the famous evangelical preachers of the day, with a Miller or a Ryle. He who had known nothing of these matters and cared less, now found himself discussing with important men whether so-and-so would be a suitable man for elevation to the episcopal bench. Though the church and the world may often be in opposition, even a church of good men can sometimes be a subtle world of its own.

He had always believed that he could preach. Now he believed that others knew that he could preach. And in the long run his new fame had this serious consequence: for the first time he began to be discontented with his lot. He looked round the two hundred parishioners of little Ketteringham and the strangers who came to sit under his ministry, and for the first time he began to wonder whether Ketteringham was not too narrow and restricted a sphere for a man of his gifts. He tried to commit these things to God, tried to be resigned. But he could not help worrying whether he should accept the parish of Wymondham if it were offered him, or St. Mary's at Bury St. Edmunds, or St. Margaret's at Ipswich, or St Peter's at Ipswich, or Beccles. None of these celebrated parishes was ever offered to him, and Ketteringham was to be the only parish of which he was ever the incumbent. But however resigned he tried to be, the contrast between his narrow duty and his public reputation afflicted him. In one disloyal moment he could not help wondering whether he failed to be offered other livings because his wife Ellen had grown into a powerful vicar's wife (as Sir John Boileau thought) and patrons were afraid of appointing her as well as himself. He tried to satisfy these wider aspirations by thinking of himself as a kind of bishop among the evangelicals of Norwich and its neighbourhood — an odd extension of his belief that he must minister to souls without minding parish boundaries. He would oversee, he determined, the godly of Wymondham and Norwich and the whole neighbourhood. It seemed to be a door out of that narrow, restricting vineyard into which the parish of Ketteringham had been suddenly metamorphosed.

It took him many years to learn that he was kicking against the pricks, and that at Ketteringham he must stay.

*　　　*　　　*　　　*　　　*

The weapon with which the crime had been committed had not been found, despite a search which dragged the moat at Stanfield Hall and ransacked every nook of Potash Farm and its outbuildings. No one knew what weapon had been used, and there was conflict among the witnesses whether the gun in the murderer's hand was a pistol or was long-barrelled. The gunmakers of London had failed to provide any evidence of a purchase by Rush.

On 21st May, a blunderbuss was found concealed in the dung-heap of an outhouse adjoining the barn at Potash Farm. The dung-heap had been searched before. It seemed extraordinary that the weapon had not been found, especially as it was lying only a foot below the surface of the manure, and close against the wall. Sir John could hardly imagine how it had escaped discovery. It was found by a labourer named Burgess, who took it to the younger Rush. The police officer Poyntz asked to see it, and having it in his hands asked leave to take it to the Chief Constable. Rush refused; whereupon Poyntz and another police officer leaped into their gig with the blunderbuss and drove away. Rush jumped upon a horse and rode after them all the way into Wymondham shouting 'Stop thief!', and at Wymondham the gig was broken.

The legal point interested Sir John. Whose property was the blunderbuss? He applied himself to Baron Parke and to Baron Rolfe, the judge who had condemned Rush and with whom Sir John had formed a friendship that would last his life. The two judges both agreed that the goods of a convicted felon belong to the Crown. But was there any doubt that the blunderbuss had belonged to Rush the felon? If there is any doubt, they replied prudently, a coroner's inquest should decide.

*　　　*　　　*　　　*　　　*

Emily Sandford, alias James, was the daughter of a lawyer's copying clerk who had married a lady above his station. She was well-educated. Sir John had much to do with her during the magistrates' examination of Rush. She told Sir John on 5th November in a private conversation that she was convinced of Rush's guilt and believed that he would have murdered her next, to ensure that her evidence should remain hidden. Sir John pitied her, but formed the lowest opinion of her character and trustworthiness. He thought she knew more about the murder than she had said. But he was distressed by her plight. She was notorious throughout the land as the mistress of a monster; how should she live, and what would happen to the unborn child? It was characteristic of him that at personal expense and inconvenience, and with no regard whatsoever for her character, he interested himself in organizing her emigration. He advised her to go to Australia.

He found that the Sandford family had a friend in Mrs. Palmer (a sister to Bradley, the housemaster at Rugby school), who lived at Victoria Road, Kensington. Emily Sandford retired to Kensington while her outfit was found, the child was born, and the ship arranged. Sir John wrote numbers of letters to plan her voyage, paid her bills, sorted her accounts, gave her a letter of identification to the bishop of Melbourne, bought her a piano so that she might earn a living in Australia by teaching music, and all for a woman who made no effort to conceal her dislike for him. She sailed for Port Philip on 17th May. Her brother Henry was drowned in Port Philip harbour, missing his footing on a gang-plank soon after their arrival; and as news of her had gone ahead, and as it had somehow leaked out that she was travelling under the assumed name of Saunders, she was rabbled by a mob on arrival at Melbourne, and found that no one would employ her. When Sir John last heard of her, she had married a German traveller and was living in Germany.

VII

AMA

AMA (her real name was Anna Maria, christened after her aunt, but everyone called her Ama) was Sir John's eldest child. She was eighteen in 1844. She kept a little, spasmodic, immature journal between 1844 and 1846; and since the daughters of Ketteringham Hall, and even Ama herself, were one day to come into friendly and respectful relations with Andrew as a man of religion, it may be of interest to transcribe some references to Andrew in her little journal. Sir John was articulate and had many informed reasons for being critical of Andrew. His daughter was not so informed and was less articulate. She often met Andrew in the houses of the poor, she taught with Sarah Cooper in the village school, and she attended his services as regularly as her father.

24 March, 1844 — 'Uncle Pollen preached a very good sermon which was such a treat after poor Mr. Andrew. We went to church again in the afternoon. Mr. A. gave us an immensely long sermon.'

(Andrew's diary, 24 March, 1844 — 'Sir John's brother [*sic*] preached in morning from Isaiah lv. 6, 7. Nothing wrong, though not directed to the heart, and ended abruptly after twenty minutes.')

14 April, 1844 — 'Mr. Andrew preached a *rigmarolist* sermon and Papa yawned a good deal.' (The subject we learn from Andrew's diary, was Jephthah's remonstrance with the king of Ammon.)

20 December, 1844 — 'Edmund drew some famous caricatures of Mr. Andrew!'

24 August, 1845 — 'To church. The Sullivans very much amused though shocked with Mr. Andrew's manner.'

7 September, 1845 — 'To church in the morning. Mr. Andrew preached very much *at us.*'

The children's attitude towards Andrew at this date is clear. They found him comic, and were faintly pitying, faintly contemptuous; and they were aware of their father's low opinion.

There is no imagination in Ama's little diary of that power in Andrew which she herself would later discern.

*   *   *   *   *

Sir John Boileau and Bishop Edward Stanley were intimate friends. They shared common interests to a high degree — art and archaeology, popular science, the education of the poor, Whig politics, and the Christian religion. Occasionally, over business matters, Sir John thought that the bishop was less decisive and effective than he might have been; he complained that the bishop had appointed Andrew to be rural dean in 1842; he found his conduct over the Barnard children more vacillating than he thought wise; and once the bishop shocked him by revealing an unsuspected toe of clay, for he grumbled to Sir John that the Whig government ought to have rewarded his political services with the archbishopric of York. Sir John admired the bishop as a man and a friend, and was vexed at this little wart of personal ambition. For the most part their friendliness was unspotted. Of all the local magnates he saw more of the bishop than anyone else, he almost always called upon him whenever he was in Norwich, and the bishop and members of his family often dined at Ketteringham.

The bishop's family of six children was older than Sir John's family. But it was natural that the younger children should be close friends with the elder Boileau children. John Boileau, the eldest son, was sent to University College, Oxford, because Arthur Stanley was a Fellow there. Mary and Catherine Stanley were intimate with Ama Boileau.

In 1844, Ama, being eighteen, came out, and on 8th November, 1845, Mrs. Stanley, who had been staying at Ketteringham, took Lady Boileau aside before she went. She warned Lady Boileau that it would be prudent not to throw Ama and Owen Stanley too much together. 'It appears clear,' she said, 'that he has serious intentions towards her.'

Owen Stanley was already carving out a career for himself in the Navy. He was applying for the command of the expedition planned to survey New Guinea and Australian waters. In the event he was given the command; and this would mean an absence of three or four years from England. Both families observed that Owen and Ama were seeing each other more than would be seemly unless there were some intention of going further. Yet it seemed imperative for Ama's sake that she should not be publicly committed to him before he sailed. She was immature; in three or four years she might meet other proposals which she should be free to consider. If the young people wanted to engage themselves, both Stanleys and Boileaus believed that they must be prevented from engaging themselves until Owen Stanley returned from Australian waters.

All this was clear to the adults. To Ama it was not clear. She loved Mrs. Stanley and the bishop, and knew enough of them to perceive that they would welcome her as a daughter. But what were Owen's feelings? She began to torture herself over him, perceiving that he behaved more warmly than would be right if he intended nothing, wondering why he came no nearer to her, why he failed to speak. How should she determine whether he failed to speak because he cared not for her, or because he had been instructed by his parents to be careful of her, as she had been instructed by her parents to be careful of him? She was torn asunder between hope that he was silent for her sake, and fear that he was silent for his own. 'I cannot feel sure,' she kept telling herself, as she looked forward to a vista of suffering years. She went with him to *The Messiah*, or danced with him at St. Andrew's Hall in Norwich. He sketched for her, and showed her the model steam-engine in his room, and came out to Ketteringham to see her act in a family play, and taught her to skate on the lake, and told her that he was getting tired of the sea and would remain only three more years in the Navy. With grief she heard her sister Caroline express doubts whether he was a man of religion. She pumped Mary Stanley about him, was grateful when Mary talked of his gentleness and his religious principles and how much he had improved during the last two years.

She knew that she loved him sincerely, yet she might not even tell the open secret to his sister Mary. Sometimes she yearned with the yearning of a girl just feeling her womanhood to throw herself into the arms of Mary or Mrs. Stanley and declare herself. But no, she told herself bitterly, a woman may love and keep all her wretchedness to herself, subject to men and their pleasure. How absurd of her parents to say that they two must not engage themselves lest she meet someone else during his absence of three years! She had engaged herself already in her own soul, she could not contemplate marrying anyone else, she had plighted her troth in the secret of her own heart, and though she had told him nothing, she had sworn to herself that she would be true to him as long as he was true to her, that she would feel herself free to marry another only if she heard news that he had engaged himself to another. It was torture, but a delicious torture which she could not bear to be without. She must see him and see him often, yet the more she saw of him the more tumultuous her breast. When they were not meeting she harassed herself whether they would soon be forbidden to meet. When they were meeting she would struggle to appear cool and afterwards be agonized that she had appeared cold or indifferent. Surely they would not prevent an *understanding* before he left England? 'I trust they will not for I feel it would be impossible for me not to *think* it whether he does or not and it would be a comfort to me to know from himself that he does love me!' Sometimes she would find him suddenly withdrawn, and wondered whether one of the parents had ordered him to see less of her.

Their meetings were agony to her, probably to them both. He could not help using affectionate language; and when she heard it she could not help tears or faintness or even shuddering. 'I hardly know what to do. Oh, it is a strange mixture of feelings; one wishes the *thing* and when it comes to the point one turns it off in a sort of agony.' They could talk of nothing but general subjects, and Ama much preferred a large company to a small circle — two people may talk to each other among twenty while among eight they must talk to the room. If he seemed cool she decided that it all seemed to be declining. He would surprise her by being hard to her brother Frank and then she wondered whether she loved him after all, at least whether she loved him enough to enable her to wait four long years. Under her pillow she put a little box which he had made for her, and often dreamed of him at night.

Owen Stanley sailed away in H.M.S. *Rattlesnake* upon that famous and successful survey which gave his name to a lofty range of mountains. Ama was left to bear the harder part — to be apparently an eligible girl and yet not to be eligible; to go perforce into company and yet to be cold to young men. She began, as was natural, to give more time to the good works of the parish, to the school and the poor. Thus she came for the first time to know Andrew as an adult.

*   *   *   *   *

Andrew had not been confident that the boys were growing as he would have them grow. The more prim among the Hall servants disapproved of the language or the conduct of the boys and reported the disapproval to the vicar. His relationship with the girls was different. For the three-quarters of the year when they were not in London they sat at his feet. They began to help, or to dominate, little Sarah Cooper and her successors in the schoolroom. Being well-instructed daughters, they visited sick parishioners, or knitted comforts for the poor. They could not avoid meeting Andrew in the parish. And meeting Andrew frequently, they could not avoid being stirred by him. He kept them upon his 'breastplate', his special list of persons for daily intercession.

Their relationships did not run smoothly. The girls honoured their father and mother, and in the main campaigns like the warfare over Sarah Cooper, they took their father's side. There were moments in these times of conflict when the vicar found them scarcely civil to him. At other times he was heartened by signs (as he supposed) of a bruised conscience. On Easter Day, 1847, preaching to a great congregation with many strangers, he observed Ama Boileau weeping, and (knowing nothing yet of Owen Stanley and his sailing) his heart lifted at these signs of penitence.

Towards the end of 1849, he began to suspect that the eldest girls sought surreptitious opportunities to converse with him. Once when he promised to visit a sick parishioner after nightfall, Caroline was waiting outside in the dark for a chance of a walk and a talk. When he met her again he gave her an envelope containing his subject for the morrow's sermon and relevant texts for study. He began to perceive in her a deep earnestness. On 2nd February, 1850, he met Ama accidentally near the school, and found her reluctant to let him go. She talked with him of the fear of death, and of feelings of misery. For the first time she seemed to the vicar to dissociate herself from her parents. She confessed indeed that she had accompanied them to a ball in Norwich a few nights before; but 'I wish it could be otherwise — I hope it will be. You are little aware how much Papa thinks of these things. He is often unhappy. You must pray for us, Mr. Andrew. I hope Caroline thinks much about religion, but she is so clever and so fond of reading that she never wants diversion in her afflictions. Agnes is much more anxious about religion'. It seemed to Andrew that the girls, though like Nicodemus they came to him by night for fear of their father, were not far from the kingdom of God.

He saw how difficult was their predicament; the social life of their household, the London season every year. The next morning he wrote a letter to Ama urging her to make an affectionate appeal to her father, asking to be allowed to withdraw from worldly amusements. He even sent her a draft of the kind of appeal which she should make. He did not realize how much he was asking. Ama sent a reply — 'I said too much; and I misled you to think my views are more decided than they really are.' It seemed evident to Andrew that she was alarmed lest her parents would hear. He sent a second note promising secrecy, and received in reply only a note from Ama declining all further correspondence. 'I fear,' said Andrew to himself, 'I must not be too forward.' He observed that she began to attend church once on Sunday instead of twice.

In 1850, the news reached England that Owen Stanley, after completing his survey in the waters of New Guinea and Australia, had been found dead at Sydney, apparently of an epileptic fit. It was natural that the girl should feel it tragically, that her attachment should for a time be heightened by the news of her loss. She fretted and became listless; and her parents likewise felt the loss of an honourable husband for Ama and of a useful connexion with a celebrated family. Andrew sent her a present of Bonar's *Night of Weeping*.

Two years later, Sir John came home from a breakfast with Macaulay and Arthur Stanley at the Hallams and was in time to receive the Reverend William Hay Gurney, who had come to ask for Ama's hand. From the worldly point of view, Gurney was as attractive as Owen Stanley. He was the son of Daniel Gurney of Runcton in Norfolk, a member of the great banking family, and was possessed of sufficient means. His mother was the daughter of the fifteenth Earl of Errol. As a younger son he was destined for the family living of North Runcton, the advowson of which his father had secured from Trinity College, Cambridge, by a private Act of Parliament in 1840. The living was held by Professor James Cumming, the eminent professor of Chemistry at Cambridge, who had been instituted as long ago as 1819, who was widely believed to be eccentric, and who was not expected to survive long. But Professor Cumming had shown no signs of dying when Willie Gurney proposed marriage to Ama, and the suitor was still a curate.

Physically it was impossible not to compare him with the upstanding figure of Owen Stanley; for Gurney was lame, from a premature birth and a paralytic stroke on the second day of his life, pathetically lame, and his face was marred by a distressing squint. He looked so frail that Sir John wondered whether he could have a reasonable expectation of life. But he was a man of high character, he was gentle and friendly and respectful, he was assured of a fitting income on his marriage; and therefore Sir John had allowed him to prosecute his suit. Two months later, on 15th July, 1852, Ama, gentle and amiable herself, told her father that she wanted to marry Mr. Gurney. The same day Sir John told him that he might propose to Ama if he waited till Monday. It was arranged that half her dowry should return to the Boileau estate if she and William had no children.

During the summer Sir John was engaged in substantial alterations to the rear part of his house, building a new corridor and other rooms; those alterations which some people think to have ruined the Tudor appearance of Ketteringham Hall. The alterations were completed only six days before the wedding.

The wedding day, 8th September, 1852, dawned fine. Sir John assembled his family and guests in the drawing-room for morning prayers, and then they all breakfasted in the newly built lower corridor. The house was prepared, even the road outside being rolled by a roller pulled by two horses; and the squire fetched the registers from the iron chest which he had provided. The bishop of Norwich (now Dr. Hinds, for Edward Stanley had died in 1849) arrived and Mr. Andrew, and together they went off to the church to arrange the service and to robe. The families went in procession from the Hall to the church, Mr. Gurney taking a sad Lady Catherine, and Sir John fetched

Ama from her room and brought her downstairs to meet the bridesmaids in the library. She was dressed in white silk with two Limerick lace flounces, a square Limerick lace veil and bouquets of clematis and orange flower. The bridesmaids (her four sisters and Willie Gurney's two sisters) were dressed in white muslin gowns, with white jackets trimmed with lace and red ribbon, and white bonnets ornamented with red verbena.

The villagers had turned out in their best clothes and were standing in a little crowd in the churchyard, and Easton, the gardener, had made arches festooned with foliage and dahlias through which the bride and her father and the bridesmaids entered the churchyard. Upon the arch at the entrance appeared the text 'God bless them.' When they arrived at the communion table, there was a din while some of the villagers entered the church and settled in the seats still unoccupied; but Sir John was delighted at the orderliness and respectfulness of his people. Bishop Hinds married them, and Andrew read the other half of the marriage service. Then William Gurney led his wife out of church, and at the porch there was a halt while the bride stopped to put on her goloshes, and ten little children, stationed outside to throw flowers, threw them a little too soon. Then the bride and bridegroom led the procession back to the Hall, Sir John escorting the bishop, and the church bells (fine bells of 1610, but newly repaired for the occasion) sounding forth. No one cheered or was noisy, but Sir John preferred it so and thought that his parishioners were showing a religious feeling and interest in the ceremony. They signed the register in the house; and then they walked about the grounds till breakfast was ready, and Sir John allowed the poor also to wander in the grounds (except upon the house terrace) and gape at their betters. Then the guests, 42 in number, sat down to the wedding breakfast, 'a princely breakfast' as the vicar thought. The bishop proposed the health of the bride and bridegroom. He paid them, and especially Ama, charming compliments with simplicity, and touched upon the Protestant religion which allowed the clergy to marry and thereby rendered them so much more useful to society and by their wives' aid so much more capable of spreading religion. William Gurney returned thanks shortly and then Ama slipped away through her father's study. After she had gone there was a plethora of speeches —

but Ama was soon ready and her father fetched her down the
great staircase into the hall where all the guests were assembled,
and they bustled her into the chariot and the bridegroom
jumped in afterwards and they galloped away to the cheers of
the guests and a little crowd of villagers waiting outside the
front door. There would have been a much larger crowd but
for an unfortunate mistake. While the breakfast was being consumed, Ringer, the gamekeeper, and Blomfield, the agent,
believed that among the people permitted to wander in the
gardens they observed two or three bad characters from
Wymondham, acting suspiciously and apparently trying to
break into the house. They sent no message into the squire but
ordered the men out of the gardens — and all the tenants
believed that they had been ordered out and started to wander
away.

At 4 o'clock everyone except Lady Catherine, who felt too
much overcome by emotion at losing her eldest daughter and
had wept bitterly as the chariot drove away, went to the White
Farm. In front of the farmhouse a long line of tables had been
erected; and now 120 poor people sat down to roast beef and
vegetables and plum pudding, Easton keeping the names and
arranging the seats. John Boileau was at one end of the long
table and Frank Boileau at the other; and the squire made a
short speech and then they all gave three cheers for Mr. and
Mrs. William Gurney and drank their health with the aid of an
eighteen-gallon cask of beer. During the meal a reporter of the
Norwich Mercury came and asked Sir John several questions,
and Sir John gave him the names of the principal guests. That
evening there was a dance in the Hall.

Sir John was delighted by the day. Everything had gone well
except for the poor being turned out of the gardens, and everyone had behaved admirably. Andrew likewise thought that the
day had been admirable. He had experienced a little jar at the
wedding breakfast, when the squire introduced him to the
guests as *my clergyman*. Andrew thanked God that he no longer
minded being introduced thus. But he was deceiving himself.
Deep within his heart he still disliked it much. He found a fierce
hope rising to the surface. 'I may live to see this proud spirit
humbled.' Like others, he had been distressed at the spectacle
of the bridegroom, thought him pitiable. He refused the fee

of £5 which the bridegroom offered him. But it was character-istic of him that he longed for a wedding of two deeper souls than he thought this union to be. Ama was amiable, he confessed it. But she was also yielding, tame, he thought her a woman of no character, she had refused to give up dancing. And William Gurney? Andrew, looking round the guests, was delighted to find among them Cunningham of Lowestoft, whom he believed to be a man of God. He found that Cunningham shared his anxieties, for Cunningham said to him, 'O sad! two semi-worldly families have mixed.'[1]

Sir John knew nothing of these meditations. He was benevolent and allowed that Andrew's sermon on that Sunday evening was a good sermon. Ama proved in the event to be as Andrew had hoped, a useful clergyman's wife at Runcton.[2] But it was not quite the last of Sir John's concern over Ama's wedding.

Nearly a month later, while he was taking the waters at Brighton, he received an anonymous letter. It said, among other charges and amid abusive language, that as a social climber he had paid heavily to have the account of the wedding inserted in the newspaper. Sir John treated this unpleasant production rightly and examined his conscience. Was it true that he had paid heavily? Quite the contrary, he had not invited reporters and had not expected them; he had only provided a list of guests at the courteous request of one reporter who was known to him, and had refused to tell him anything of the speeches. Was the intention of the poison pen simply to

[1] There is a story of the unworldly character of Mr. Cunningham of Lowestoft in A. J. C. Hare's book *The Gurneys of Earlham* (vol. ii, p. 257). 'One day when he was reading family prayers, a servant burst in with "Please, sir, your study's on fire." "All right James," said Mr. Cunningham very quietly, "but this is not the time to speak of such things", and reverently and deliberately he went on reading the chapter and the prayers which followed to the end. The study was completely burnt, but the fire did not spread to the rest of the house.' Mrs. Cunningham was a Gurney and a sister of Elizabeth Fry. Mr. Cunningham died on 1st August, 1863.

[2] Professor Cumming at last died on 10th October, 1861, about a quarter of an hour before the beginning of the morning service at Runcton. Daniel Gurney came into the vestry immediately after the service and said to his son, 'The living is yours!'

wound his feelings? Yes. Was he in fact, he asked himself, a social climber? He was not sure, as he examined his conscience, that he could give an absolute negative to the question. He was sure, at least, that the poison pen was exaggerating.

Sir John's spirit could not be humbled (if Andrew was right in supposing that this was what his spirit needed) by false and abusive letters. He was unmoved. But it was not to be long before he was humbled, and in a way that none could foresee.

VIII

THE COFFINS

LADY CATHERINE had always been delicate, frequently under remedies. She could not walk far, nor exert herself. She would take fresh air in the carriage or strolling in the garden, and in the house she was quiet. Epidemically she suffered from a troublesome cough which made her husband and others afraid that her chest was weak. In March, 1853, she alarmed her husband further by beginning to spit blood when she coughed. Dr. Scott thought that she was suffering from bronchitis, not from tuberculosis, and that the blood came from the throat, not from the lungs. Her throat was found to be inflamed and ulcerated, her stomach became dyspeptic. All that summer, with small variations for better or for worse, the cough persisted. Her husband was afraid and distressed at her weakness, and found himself offended with his children or his friends if they treated the malady lightly. A visit to take the waters at Brighton Spa during July and August seemed to make her stronger, and for a time he lost his fear. There was talk of sending her abroad to winter at Nice. But on 23rd August he caused her to be examined by the London specialist, Sir James Clarke. Clarke judged more gravely of Lady Catherine's condition than any of the general practitioners. He told Sir John that she was in a precarious state and was unfit to travel to Nice. His manner, almost more than his words, gave Sir John the impression that she would not improve. On 24th August he travelled with Lady Catherine back to Ketteringham, taking a carriage without arms to the seats so that he could lay her flat, and feeling that he was taking her thither for the last time and that he could do little now but watch and comfort her end. He asked Caroline, whom he called 'Carry' (since Ama's wedding the eldest daughter at home), the capable, stern, decisive Caroline, to act as her mother's deputy in the house.

His mind turned to burial. A few months before he had

attended the interment of one of the Havilands in the family vault at Fen Ditton. He felt it appropriate that a squire and his family should be buried in the chancel vault at the squire's church. Just as it was fitting that the squire as father of the parish should sit in a special pew in the congregation, it was fitting that he and his should receive a special place at their latter end. He knew that beneath the chancel at Ketteringham church was an old vault, the resting place, it might be presumed, of the remains of some of those great families — Greys or Heveninghams or Atkyns — who once had been squires of Ketteringham. When he purchased the advowson of the living with the estate, he had been given the key of the vault. A week after he had received the diagnosis of Sir James Clarke upon his wife, he rose early, took Hunter, the Scottish carpenter, with him, and went to perform before breakfast, unobserved, the solemn and sad duty of examining the vault.

Hunter unlocked the vault and clambered down the steps into its bowels. He reported that it was filled with old coffins and there was scarcely room for one coffin more. One of the coffins was derelict and burst open. He could find only one coffin with a name inscribed upon it — Heron Esq., April 1st, 1702. Sir John himself refrained from descending, but stood at the head of the steps peering down into the crowded space below. He asked whether the vault could be enlarged. The carpenter meditated long upon the possibility and then answered that he was afraid not, for the foundations of the church would not allow it.

For a time Sir John thought about the problem, but a resolution was slowly forming in his mind.

Lady Catherine was sometimes better, but she frequently alarmed him; and when she alarmed him, he could hardly sleep or think of anything else in his anxiety. On 15th September, finding her better, he travelled to London on business, only to receive that evening a telegram from Ketteringham to say that Lady Catherine had been attacked by spasms, apparently brought on by mixing her medicine with the porter and port wine which she successively drank at lunch. The last train for Wymondham left at 8.45 p.m. With James, the postman, he reached Shoreditch station at midnight to ask for a special train. The station was closed. He found a porter and another under man, who told him that he could not start for two hours as they would need to bring an engine from Stratford and to telegraph all down the line to ensure safety; that there were five luggage trains upon the line and that he might be delayed or even suffer an accident; and finally that the cost would be £46. He waited for the morning train. On the 18th, after a medicinal dinner of partridge and bitter ale, she was again seized with spasms, rapid and violent. Sir John believed that she was gradually losing strength, that these attacks would recur, each attack lowering her further, until the end came.

She was much the more cheerful of the two. He fussed around her, rejoicing at every little pleasure which she was able to feel, delighted when she sat up in her chair, calm and pure, and looked out of her windows over the water of the lake to the distant trees, turning russet in the late September sunshine. His prayers were now an agitated agony on her behalf. Two days later he again conversed with the carpenter about the vault. By 16th October he was speaking to his son John of 'our family vault'; and on or about 24th October, 1853, he sat down and wrote the fatal letter to Dr. Hinds, the bishop of Norwich.

He had consulted his old tutor, Mr. Bickmore of Hethel, upon his plans. Would it be wrong, he asked, to apply for leave to remove the coffins in Ketteringham vault to a grave in the churchyard and to appropriate the vault for his own family? The coffins, he had said, belong to a family which lived here 150 years ago and was now extinct; no one's feelings can be hurt. Bickmore saw no objection; and therefore Sir John wrote the same request to the bishop of Norwich, asking whether he might empty the vault and appropriate it, and suggesting that if there was any doubt upon the point he might consult Mr. Kitson, the ecclesiastical lawyer.

Bishop Hinds was already poorly from that illness of the bladder which at last would force him so prematurely to resign his see. He liked and admired Sir John; and because he had risen from comparatively humble circumstances, he perhaps respected Sir John's rank and position more than the aristocratic Bishop Stanley had done. Perhaps, like everyone else, he was a little afraid of Sir John. He believed that the request was illegal; but he did not see who was to protest against its illegality and therefore encouraged him, on 26th October, with a *pecca fortiter* letter:

My dear Sir John,

Your legal right to remove the coffins would, I think be questionable, if there were any to question it. This does not seem likely. I can only advise you as a friend, and my advice is, quietly to transfer to the churchyard, all the coffins except that which has a name on it. It will be necessary, however, that you should first obtain the vicar's consent for the use of the churchyard, and he may, perhaps, claim a fee such as is demanded for the removal of a coffin from the churchyard of one parish to that of another. In the latter case the removal is made under a faculty from the ordinary, the application for it being from the friends or representatives of the deceased. As you do not appear in that capacity, I doubt whether I could grant a faculty and think, on the whole, that the matter had better be conducted privately and quietly.

With our kind regards

Fortified by this approval of the highest ecclesiastical authority that the plan was illicit but might be carried out surreptitiously, Sir John determined to act.

On 31st October, he was just about to set out for Hethersett to see the vicar and secure his permission, but was prevented by the arrival of Dr. Gibson to see Lady Catherine. It was the second fatal step. For it meant that he first introduced the subject to Andrew in writing and not in conversation, and the ensuing misunderstanding was calamitous.

On Tuesday, 1st November, Sir John determined, with the doctor's encouragement, to take Lady Catherine for a few days to lodgings in Lowestoft. But first he attended a wedding in Ketteringham church. Two cottagers, Eliza Osborne and William Ireland, were married by Andrew, in the presence of all four parents, whom the squire had particularly requested to attend, and of Sir John and his daughters. He was anxious that parents in the parish should learn to attend their children's weddings and gave them a hot pie and some beer for the wedding feast, and sent Easton, while the service was proceeding, to put an American clock as a present in their cottage. Just before the beginning of the marriage service he had a letter delivered to

Andrew. The letter explained that he wished to empty the vault and appropriate it, that he had the bishop's sanction, and asked permission. He also asked that Andrew might call at the Hall immediately after the end of the service as Sir John was setting out for Lowestoft. Andrew excused himself from coming at once, but opened the letter, read it through, and said that he would send an answer. And so Sir John and family drove away in the great berlin to Norwich station.

Andrew was accustomed to think Sir John high-handed, but he was staggered at the high-handedness of the proposal now before him. No one had been buried in the vault since he had become the incumbent. But he knew the parish well enough to be aware of its recent history, and he had owed the benefice to the connection between his wife's family and the Atkyns family. Both he and his wife were aware that the vault had been used for burials within living memory, and indeed for the burial of the near relatives of persons now living. They supposed that the squire must be as aware of these facts as themselves. They had no idea that Sir John supposed the bodies to have been buried 150 years before, and to belong to extinct families. It seemed to Andrew, and still more to Mrs. Andrew, that the squire in his passion for rule and possession was intending to commit an act of sacrilege. Yet he claimed that he had the bishop's sanction for the act.

Andrew worried how he should reply. It seemed impossible to ask the bishop whether in fact any sanction had been given. He consulted Day, the rector of Hethersett, and Sharpe, the vicar of Cromer. They agreed in recommending him to consult the archdeacon, and accordingly Andrew wrote to inquire of Archdeacon Bouverie. But before he could receive a reply, Sir John had returned from Lowestoft, looked for the reply and, not finding it, rode over to Hethersett to interview Andrew.

Why, he demanded, had he received no reply to his letter? Andrew told him that he had written to consult the archdeacon. Sir John was not pleased. 'I am sorry for that. I wanted to keep the matter very private, or it will probably reach the ears of my daughters or Lady Catherine, who must feel that it is owing to her state that I am endeavouring to prepare the vault and would occasion much pain and perhaps do harm also to her shattered frame'.

'It was only as a formality,' said Andrew meekly, 'and because I think it due to the archdeacon officially.'

'Then you do not yourself see any objection?'

'Oh, no,' said Andrew. He was afraid to say that he did.

'Then we can, I think, determine the matter at once, for I have a letter from the bishop which advises that it should be done privately and quietly and with your consent.'

Sir John read aloud the important parts of the bishop's letter.

'Oh yes,' was all that Andrew could reply.

'But I ought to pay you a fee for breaking the grave in the churchyard. What should it be?'

Andrew did not know.

'As it seems only an acknowledgment, will a sovereign be right?'

Sir John took out his purse, extracted a sovereign, and laid it upon the table. And now Andrew was at last able to make a suggestion. It seemed to him that as this terrible act must be perpetrated, it were best concealed. 'I think,' he said, 'the removal should take place after dusk, to avoid curiosity.' Sir John agreed. He asked Andrew to write to Archdeacon Bouverie that they had settled it all and to beg him to take no further notice of the matter. Andrew said that he would.

Sir John rose to go. Andrew said, 'I hope you will take care other graves are not disturbed in burying the coffins.'

'I will. Is there any particular spot you prefer?'

They talked it over, and agreed upon a spot near the squire's palings, twelve yards south-east of the south-east corner of the chancel.

They walked together to the door and the squire mounted his horse. Andrew stood by the stirrup and said, 'Will you write to Archdeacon Bouverie instead of me? You know him well, I do not.'

'I have not time; I am obliged to go off this afternoon to London.'

Andrew pressed his request, and so Sir John agreed, and rode away to a short meeting of magistrates in Hethersett, and thence to Ketteringham Hall. Andrew walked back into the house and saw the sovereign lying upon the table. He could not think what to do with it. Freed from the inarticulate condition brought by Sir John's powerful presence, he fancied that by means of the sovereign Sir John was tricking him into being a fellow-conspirator in the plot. If he kept it, he might seem to be an accomplice. If he returned it, he was afraid that Sir John would suppose him to think the fee inadequate and therefore to be a covetous man. It seemed easier to keep it.

Sir John believed that all the proprieties had now been observed. He possessed the sanction of the bishop and the consent of the vicar, he had paid the requisite fee, and he had agreed with the vicar the place of interment. The vicar himself had suggested that it should be done after dark. When Sir John arrived home, he saw with satisfaction Lady Catherine going out in her bath chair, and summoned Easton, the head gardener, and Hunter, the Scottish carpenter. He gave orders that they and their men should remove the bodies that evening; that everything should be done respectfully and carefully. He went with Easton to the churchyard and showed him the spot of interment. Then he returned to the Hall and wrote to the archdeacon that he need do nothing now, as all was settled. 'I think it must be,' he wrote in his journal. 'Once the coffins (are) removed this night I do not know who is to put them back again, or who can call me to account, and I hope I have also done it all wisely and discreetly and decently.' In the late afternoon he caught the London train at Wymondham, still thinking of it. It disturbed him a little that the bodies must be interred after dark, as though the deed were in some way disreputable. But he justified the time to himself because Catherine and the girls might be distressed if they heard that a family grave were being prepared, and it would be better that the idlers of the village should not stand watching.

The same Saturday he returned to Ketteringham, and was delighted to find his wife better. On Sunday morning, 13th November, he went to church.

The Andrews had arrived at church earlier. It had been reported to them that the stench in the church was insufferable. The long-pent odour of death, released after so many years, hung about the pews like a miasma. They fetched chloride of lime to purify the atmosphere before the congregation assembled. Mrs. Andrew could not conceal her passion at what had been done. As the people came to church and Sir John among them, she saw Easton and Hunter, and made a violent attack upon them in public. The matter could not be hid. Before many hours had passed, the entire village knew what had been done.

Sir John was but mildly perturbed. He had long ago formed an unfavourable opinion of Mrs. Andrew. He did not mind if the village knew the secret provided that his wife and daughters were ignorant. He was much more concerned that day with pleasure at taking his wife to evening prayer. It was the first time for many months that she had been able to accompany him to church. Easton and Hunter next day showed him the place of interment, and told him how there had been five coffins in the vault. They had found other names besides that of Mr. Heron. The coffin of Lady Mary Heveningham was found in ruins and with its contents scattered. Sir John was glad to hear that his plan had therefore done good to the church. He could not help a little qualm from time to time. He kept reminding himself that he had the bishop's, the vicar's and (as he had now learnt) the archdeacon's approval. He also had the approval of the churchwardens — being himself and his agent, Mr. Blomfield. He ordered his builders to prepare four stones to mark the corners of the new grave.

On the morning of 23rd November, he rode out with his daughter Agnes. He returned to the Hall and found awaiting him a letter from a Mr. Pemberton of Bourn Hall, Caxton, in Cambridgeshire. He had not before received a letter couched in such language.

Sir,
I learn this morning, with the deepest surprise and indignation, that you have ventured to break open the family vault at Ketteringham and directed that the coffins should be all placed in a hole dug by your direction, somewhere in the churchyard. As one of those coffins contains the remains of my sister-in-law, I lose not a post in writing to request an immediate explanation of this most extraordinary proceeding — and I will at once avow to you that should my information prove but too true I shall do my best to seek reparation by law for a conduct so utterly outrageous, so utterly devoid of the feelings either of a gentleman or a Christian . . .

Sir John was shocked at the letter. Pemberton must be married to one of the Atkyns family, perhaps to a sister of Miss

Peach. Instead of moving the coffins of an extinct family, he appeared to have moved those of a family still flourishing and therefore to have wounded deeply the feelings of the living. He was most sorry for the sake of the Atkyns family. But he saw also the peril of his own reputation and standing. If legal proceedings ensued, the story could be made to look black; and he could not defend himself adequately, if the story became public property, without appealing to the bishop. He shrank from such an appeal, partly because he would infallibly annoy the bishop, and partly because he had disregarded the bishop's advice to leave the coffin with a name upon it. He knew that he had enemies close at hand, remembered the anonymous letter after Ama's wedding, and was aware that there would be tongues ready to portray the interment in lurid colours. 'I will endeavour to answer gently and truly, and hope it may all be soothed.' He did not see how the news could be kept from his wife and daughters, and that evening told them gently, by little and little, the simple facts. They were not distressed.

On 24th November, he drafted an answer to Mr. Pemberton. But he could hardly sleep that night, and next day took his letter into Norwich to discuss it with Mr. Evans, the chancellor of the diocese. If the case came to law, it would come before Mr. Evans as chancellor, and the interview was therefore perhaps improper. But Mr. Evans treated Sir John with consideration, professed to understand how it had been done in error and without intending wrong, said that the expressions in Mr. Pemberton's letter were most violent but thought that in the end all would come right. He offered certain emendations to Sir John's letter to Mr. Pemberton, and as revised the substance of the letter ran thus:

Sir John described Lady Catherine's illness, and how he had believed that all the coffins were as old as 1702; that he had consulted 'proper persons' and received the permission of the vicar who had been paid a fee; that all things had been done with decency and propriety; that four stones were being prepared to mark the grave. 'It was not till I got your letter that I had any idea that there was any coffin such as that you name, nor that of any person related to those now alive. Had I known this, or felt that I could pain the feelings of any living person, I beg to assure you I would have suffered any distress myself for want of the vault rather than have occasioned it. I will only add that the state of the vault for health and safety made it desirable something should be done with the coffins and that it never occurred to me, nor apparently to those whom I consulted, that irreverence would be shown to the dead by the coffins being removed to the churchyard.'

By 26th November, the matter was becoming widely known. Wherever he went, Sir John met people who had heard of it. Thrower, the Ketteringham blacksmith, was heard to declare hotly in the midst of a drinking bout that he would be revenged on the squire for removing his old friends' coffins. Mrs. Andrew, thoroughly roused, had visited the cottages of Mrs. Blomfield and Miss Beasley and talked about Sir John's shocking conduct. She went with Miss Beasley into the schoolroom and in the presence of all the children was heard declaring, 'I will not submit to him — I will write myself to the archbishop of Canterbury.' On 30th November, she wrote one of her fierce letters to Sir John himself, couched in the third person. The dean of Norwich, Mr. Pellew, received an angry letter from Mrs. Pemberton. Archdeacon Bouverie received a violent letter from Miss Norgate, who lived opposite Mr. Andrew in Hethersett, had an evil reputation as the village gossip, and was one of the strangers who habitually attended Ketteringham church; she demanded that the archdeacon inquire into the outrage committed upon the feelings of inhabitants of Ketteringham and of the neighbouring villages. Even in Wymondham ballads were being composed in the public houses; neighbouring villagers began to salute the inhabitants of Ketteringham with the jeer, 'Are you one of the body-snatchers?' Popular gossip talked of it as the resurrection case, and Sir John Boileau was frequently described in the taverns as 'Resurrection Jack'. Caroline Boileau, teaching her little class of boys in the Sunday school, told them innocently that God alone can raise the dead from their graves, and was vexed to find that they all burst into laughter. 'If murder had been committed,' said Mr. Bickmore to Sir John, 'more odium could not have been excited.'

According to the popular version, the squire had known that his recent predecessors were buried in the vault; secretly and by moonlight he and his men had crept into the church, sacrilegiously emptied the vault and jumbled the remains irreverently in a common grave; all this had been done without the vicar's permission or knowledge; the crime was only betrayed by the stench when the congregation came to church. It was impossible for Sir John to write to the papers explaining what had happened. Though he went round diligently calling upon his friends and giving them the true version, even summoning Lofty, the constable, into his study to show him the letters, and handing the letters round at Quarter Sessions, his utmost diligence could not overtake rumour on her wings. Not all the persons upon whom he called were friendly. Lady Hoste was mortally offended against him. He made the mistake of calling with his daughter Caroline upon the Norgates at Hethersett, and endured a most disagreeable scene with Miss Norgate — 'really like an insane person and quite offensive if I had not determined not to be offended — almost positively declining to believe anything I said and evidently is the person who has written to and excited by her false statements Miss Atkyns'. Miss Norgate, when not saying sharp things aloud, went on muttering. Why, she demanded, had he not gone himself to ascertain personally who had been buried there? 'If you had asked anybody they could have told you some of the coffins were recent. Mr. Andrew knew quite well.'

'Then why did he not tell me?'

'Oh,' said Miss Norgate, 'he was afraid.'

'But why? And how does this alter my position of ignorance, whatever his reason? But,' he added, and Caroline agreed, 'I do not believe he knew it.'

He found this attempt to catch up with the gossip humiliating. The attitude and manner of his neighbours towards him became less respectful. In mid-December an article, veiled but patent to everyone who had heard the rumour, appeared in the *Norfolk Chronicle*. Sir John went to see the proprietor, and ensured that nothing further should appear improperly and without his consent. In the following week the editor applied for permission to insert a fresh article, better informed. Sir John thought it wiser to wait to see if further public comment appeared before he consented to any insertion. An unknown woman had invaded Jarrold's office and attacked the editor for failing to include articles sent to him. But Mr. Clarke, the solicitor, undertook to see the editor of the *Norfolk News*. Mr.

Evans, the chancellor of the diocese, saw Jarrold's editor and stopped him inserting anything, and the editor of the *Chronicle* undertook to deal with the editor of the *Bury Post*. In spite of these precautions, a letter appeared in the *Examiner*, mentioning Sir John by name.

Mr. Pemberton, in a second letter of 29th November, demanded that the coffins be restored to the vault and in the presence of a member of his family. Sir John was aware that a restoration under these conditions must be his humiliation. He consulted Blomfield and Easton, who were vehemently opposed to restoration. The vault, they said, had been unsafe and insanitary. Sir John suggested to his friends that he should make reparation by bricking up the vault and putting a railing round the place of interment. But he knew that he must do everything to repair the feelings of the ladies whom he had so sorely wounded; and since Mr. Pemberton was inexorable, he agreed that the coffins should be restored to the vault. He asked the dean of Norwich, as the friend of both parties, to manage the whole unpalatable affair.

On 13th December, therefore, a solemn procession restored the coffins to the vault. Sir John was not present — he had departed to stay with Lord Hastings at Melton Constable. Andrew thought that he was not present because he could not bear this final humiliation. On the contrary, his absence was the final humiliation. Mr. Pemberton insisted that Sir John be not there, and the dean of Norwich had persuaded him, though with extreme reluctance, to consent.

Mr. Cundall, the Norwich undertaker, watched by Mr. Pemberton, the dean of Norwich, Mr. Andrew, Mr. Clarke (Sir John's solicitor), and Mr. Blomfield, the agent, restored the coffins to their old home, beginning at eleven o'clock in the morning and finishing about three o'clock in the afternoon. Some neighbouring villagers wished to witness the occasion, but were prevented from entering the churchyard by a superintendent of police and his constables. The church was filled with workmen, the floor was covered with straw, the heavy coffins were placed on trucks and trundled to their destination. Then the vault was bricked up, the steps filled with mould, and the top (the entrance being just on the left of the church stove) was paved over.

The dean managed the proceedings with courtesy and charity, and even Mr. Pemberton softened towards the absent Sir John. Mr. Pemberton eyed Andrew with disfavour, regarding him as a kind of accomplice, and Andrew was not pleased with his manner. The dean was silently supposed by Andrew to be 'a thorough Sir John's man'; whereas Sir John was silently supposing the dean to be too ready to give Mr. Pemberton all that he wanted. The path of the arbiter is ever stony.

Mr. Pemberton now wanted more than the restoration of the coffins. He had discovered that the monument to Mr. Peach had been moved by Sir John from its place on the chancel walls, when the chancel was decorated, to make room for a history of Sir John's family. He demanded that the Peach monument be replaced, and Sir John's friends advised him that the removal had been illegal and that he must agree. On 27th December, Hunter and another changed over the two monuments.

*   *   *   *   *

It will readily be understood that during December, 1853, the tension between squire and vicar was sharper than ever before. Andrew himself was little changed. 'May I never reproach but pity and pray for him . . . O that his disappointments may humble him. How will he next meet me? I have ever said, I dread nothing but his kindness. Just before this occurred he sent some game and I expressed my fears there was something afloat.' On a night in January he dreamed that he was in the vestry on Sunday when Sir John entered and fell upon his neck and wept. 'Is it an intimation of our future amicable feeling? Shall I ever see that poor man a penitent?'

While Andrew interceded for Sir John as earnestly as ever before, Sir John's attitude to Andrew could not help but change. The Andrews might have averted the calamity. If Mrs. Andrew had not been so hostile to him, she would have come and said a kind word. Had Andrew known that bodies had recently been buried in the vault and been afraid to say so? 'Either they knew,' said Sir John, 'when he consented to the removal of the coffins and took a fee for doing so . . or he did not. If the former, how could he not mention it, and let us both fall into the error? If he did not, how wrong to turn upon me, and for her to make all the excitement and rouse public feeling instead of at once informing me . . . I do not see how we can hold any intercourse in future — at least till time has softened feelings.' He was rash enough to write to Andrew, on 6th December, a friendly and humble letter which complained about the conduct of his wife. Andrew did not reply. Mrs. Andrew sent one of her third-person letters to Sir John and the letter did nothing to further harmony. It seemed, moreover, an injustice that the vicar should receive a fee of a sovereign for displacing the bodies, and another fee of five guineas for the privilege of restoring them.

For the first time in the long history of his worship at Ketteringham church, Sir John wondered whether he could bear to attend morning service. Would he be able to go without sin when he so vehemently disapproved of the conduct of the vicar's wife? On Sunday, 4th December, he spent time composing himself into a mood of forgiveness before he went. He went again on 11th December, 'trusting I have no ill-will to my clergyman or his mis-guided party'. He went — but that day he ordered his daughters to give no assistance in the Sunday School.

On Christmas Day, which this year fell upon a Sunday, he went to the morning service, and found under his nose in the pew a sealed letter from Mr. Andrew. His devotions during the service were disturbed. He was afraid that the letter contained some new cause of squabble. He showed it to his son John, who wanted him to leave it unopened in the pew. But he reflected that on a Sunday, and a Christmas Day, and when he had just announced the Sacrament for the following Sunday, Mr. Andrew would scarcely engage in bitterness and controversy. He determined to take the letter home with him and to assume that it contained nothing wrong. When he reached the Hall, he took John and Frank and the letter to his room, and nervously opened it in their presence. It contained a list of texts for Mr. Andrew's sermons during the coming year.

Vicar and squire did not meet socially until 2nd February, 1854. They happened to pay a simultaneous visit to Miss Beasley, the schoolmistress, who was ill. Both men have left descriptions of the encounter. Andrew wrote, 'I was visiting Beasley when he entered and no person could have discerned any interruption of (his usual term) our friendship.' Sir John recorded, 'Walked to Miss Beasley . . . and there met suddenly Mr. Andrew, who *delighted* to see me . . . I should have had my say with him but Miss Beasley almost fainting, and unwilling to agitate her.'

Thereafter, their relations were outwardly normal. And yet it seemed to Andrew that the positions of the two men had perceptibly changed. The policy of submission no longer appeared appropriate; had indeed contributed to the disaster. In October, 1854, at the first harvest festival, Andrew consciously abandoned that policy. Sir John requested that there should be only one prayer. 'I however commenced my future mode of conduct . . . I have found my past yielding everything has not brought peace. Henceforth I shall act with distinctness and decision.' He read two prayers.

*   *   *   *   *

Sir John was not to be diverted by these events from securing a proper burial for his family. It seemed to him somehow inappropriate that the squire's family should be buried in a *grave*; it was appropriate that they should be buried in a *vault*, and he had been excluded from the vault which he regarded as his own. He turned to investigating the possibility of constructing a vault in the churchyard. He took every possible precaution that nothing could be challenged, a long succession of legal opinions. It was found better to construct a mausoleum above ground in the churchyard. A faculty was secured, the design (almost a copy of Mr. Bevan's mausoleum in Nunhead cemetery) was approved by the lawyers. The mausoleum was erected by Lofty, the stonemason of Hethersett, its place in the graveyard selected, and Andrew's approval sought. Andrew was paid a fee of £25 for this construction. It stands there today, with its rusty lock and double doors of metal, a pallid dingy green, gloomily overshadowed by the great chestnut trees, pathetic amongst the long weeds and the unkept grass and the clutter of gravestones; but not trivial nor mean, to him who has the eye of history and can see behind the last century, far behind, to the Provost who ruled Paris while Saint Louis called the warriors to his ill-fated crusade.

IX

CHARLES

IN 1854, there was a bumper harvest, estimated at one-fifth above average. The squire and the vicar agreed to give the poor a dinner by public subscription, and the vicar agreed to read a prayer. The harvest festival was to replace the frolics in public houses. It was the only important occasion when Andrew's path crossed the path of Sir John's youngest son, Charles.

*   *   *   *   *

It was a tragedy of the parish that Sir John, having no confidence in the religious instruction of his vicar, tried to keep his children away from him. His sons were prepared for confirmation at school, his daughters were prepared for confirmation in London during the season. But the daughters, being at home, could not be removed from the vicar's preaching, and sooner or later all of them fell in some measure under his influence. The sons, being rarely at home, rarely encountered him. And perhaps they would have been less likely to be influenced if they had met him more frequently. Of the educated, it was women rather than men who felt the power in Andrew's words.

Sir John was a devoted parent. But in the eyes of his children he was so old-fashioned as to be sometimes tyrannical. He continued to expect from them, when they were adults, the same unyielding respect and obedience which had been exacted in their childhood. He had the keenest sense of gentlemanly behaviour. He watched, even fussed, over their conduct, and was pained, sometimes beyond measure, by the barbarous behaviour of the adolescent or the young adult. He found it difficult to understand or to make allowances, and was less capable than most parents of transferring his children from subjects into friends, that classical awkwardness of parenthood. His younger children were in a manner motherless. For Lady Catherine, after her long series of pregnancies, fell into that invalid state which lasted from 1839 till her death; and the children were educated, under the distant and forbidding eye of their father, by Mr. Bickmore, the tutor, and by a series of governesses. They all developed strong wills, in their different ways. Of the nine children, Ama, the eldest, was perhaps the only one with whom their father never came into open conflict.

Growing up was easier for the girls than the boys. The weaker sex has its own inimitable ways of winning the conflict; the boy cannot use the weapons of the woman in his quest for independence. It is symbolic that in the most famous of Victorian conflicts between father and child — the Barretts of Wimpole Street — it was a daughter who claimed her freedom.

The rules of the household at Ketteringham impinged upon the boys as they became adults. Perhaps they half-resented, at times, being driven to the sermon every Sunday morning, or the regimen of sermon-reading and family prayers on Sunday evenings. They grew up in boarding-schools, and their conception of civilized behaviour was not always their father's. Sir John would not permit smoking in Ketteringham Hall. If a guest smoked during his stay in the house, he was never invited again. The boys had inevitably acquired, if not the habit of smoking, at least the conviction that it was not wrong for a young man, and they perhaps felt, at times, that they would never be independent adults until their right to smoke at home was conceded. But it seems to have been impossible to argue upon such matters with their father.[1]

Again, all four boys, at Oxford or in the services, contracted debts. Their father moved in the circles of the wealthy, the boys were brought up to associate with the children of wealthy parents. Yet their father had strict, almost puritan ideas of economy, he kept them upon the smallest of allowances, he was

[1] It should be remembered that Sir John was not exceptional for those days. Bishop Murray, interviewing Edward Vesey Bligh for ordination in 1855, said 'Yes, it is true I have appointed Mr. — to Wouldham. But oh! *if I had only known* — what do you think? — why that when he came here the other day to be instituted he actually smoked in his bedroom! — *he would never* have had that living.' (Bligh's autobiography, in Wingfield-Stratford, *This was a man*, Robert Hale, 1949, p. 143).

uneasily aware of the eight other children for whom he must provide. They therefore ran up bills, found themselves in debt to an extent which they dare not disclose to their father, in the inevitable calamity of ultimate discovery were tempted towards petty deceits like concealing part of the debt; and thus poisoned for the time the relation between father and son.

With the two elder boys — John the heir, and Frank, destined in the event to succeed to the baronetcy and to Ketteringham Hall — this mode of education was not disastrous. They grew beyond their not extensive debts, and each carried out a modest career of independence, the one as secretary to Lord John Russell, the other as a barrister with a moderate little practice.

The two younger boys, Edmund and Charles, moved on the contrary from disaster to disaster. In both boys there was a weakness of character difficult to attribute only to the mode of their upbringing. It is possible that both suffered from an instability needing the kind of treatment which neither the education nor the medical science of that age were qualified to give. Edmund, after a chequered course in the Royal Navy, disappeared abroad and for years on end was lost to the sight of his family. But these bare facts give no idea of the agonies and distress of spirit which they caused within Ketteringham Hall.

But our concern is with the youngest boy, Charles Boileau.

Charles had been expelled from Eton, transferred to Rugby, and expelled from Rugby. He was a gentle, poetic, affectionate soul who wrote verses and struggled against temptation with repeated earnestness and utter failure. He was always professing good resolutions and always professing them sincerely. Apart from his mother, whom he loved dearly, he was closest in affection to Caroline. At the age of twenty, on 2nd September, 1853, he was gazetted as an ensign in the 50th Foot.

Three months later, with Charles away with his regiment, a painful letter arrived from the adjutant ordering him to pay the washerwoman's bill at Plymouth. In the early part of 1854, Charles seems to have written a hard and impertinent letter home, and his father consulted with his lawyer about casting him off from the family. On 2nd October, 1854, a letter arrived from Charles, now at Portsmouth, saying that he expected a court-martial for his debts, and that unless the debts were cleared it would be the end of his army career.

Sir John sent the two eldest sons Frank and John, to Portsmouth, to discover whether Charles was truly penitent or was acting penitence to gain money; and also to try to stop legal proceedings until the family had a chance to intervene. Sir John hoped that if possible they might get him sent abroad. The news of the impending court-martial arrived at Ketteringham on the same day as the news of the battle of the Alma. Sir John hoped that, with so many officers killed or wounded in the Crimea, Charles might even be required to go there; and if not required to go, perhaps his father's influence might arrange that he be ordered to go. It was possible that active service might change Charles' character; and if therefore he could be ordered abroad, Sir John said that he would pay all his debts, provide him with an outfit, and thus offer him a fresh start.

Never had Sir John's local duties as a Norfolk magnate seemed so overwhelming. While John and Frank were away at Portsmouth, and Sir John could hardly think of anything but Charles, he remembered that he must prepare his speech for the annual meeting of the Agricultural Association. He found that his mind was so harassed, he could not think clearly about agriculture or even keep a regular train of thought in the mind, for his thoughts kept darting away to his anxieties, to Charles or Edmund or his wife's health, or his own failing powers, or the incompetence of his manager and the embarrassments of running his estate. His speech was a failure. He lost the thread, became confused, forgot the argument in support of the Association, but waded on and hoped that he had not made the audience greatly uncomfortable. He rode home, exhausted, to lunch; and after the meal John and Frank returned from Portsmouth.

They reported that Charles was drinking, and using reckless means to keep himself afloat. Was he penitent? They said he was very miserable, not merely because the duns were pestering him, and that he was disgusted with himself. The mess had a bill against him for £90, and the commander, a distant relative of the Boileaus, had agreed to postpone a report of the complaint in the hope that Charles might be ordered to the Crimean war. 'What am I to do,' agonized Sir John, 'if he is not soon sent out?

The Lord God omniscient guide my decision for his eternal good and enable me to look to that more than his present worldly prospects, if I cannot combine them.'

Charles had asked if he might come to Ketteringham. 'But how can I take him in, smoking (as I believe), drinking certainly and admitting he has no control over his own actions ... bring misery within this sanctuary and draw the dishonour closer upon us, and where it must stick upon all the family if he did ill here? I hope I forgive him but he has not returned to me the penitent son. He is in difficulties and wants to get out of them... but I hear of no grief for us — no sense of penitence to God or his parents — but is reckless and hopeless and declares (himself) incapable of any exertion. How can I look upon him or consent to bring him to my home, to his mother and his sisters ... How can I bring him home?'

He sent John back to Portsmouth. And on 20th October, a merciful letter arrived. Charles had been ordered out to Turkey within ten days, with a detachment of the Rifles. His father at once agreed to pay all his debts. Should he allow him home to see his mother before he sailed to the war? On 23rd October, he met a morose and taciturn Charles at the lawyer's chambers in London and brought him down in the train to Ketteringham that evening.

The 24th was the harvest festival. With all the Boileau family including Charles, and all the Andrew family, 170 parishioners assembled at the church. The seating was just adequate to these numbers. After the short service the congregation moved out to a sort of booth or tent, manufactured with sail cloths or tarpaulins from the railway, spread out from the carpenter's shed. The poor sat in their families, and after Andrew (at the squire's invitation) said grace, they consumed the inevitable roast beef, potatoes and plum pudding (there were thirty plum puddings) and ale — two pints of beer for a man or woman and one pint for a child. The cost of the dinner was £12, of which Sir John had contributed £6 and Andrew £3.

After the final grace, and the 'Gloria' chanted by Andrew, Sir John made a little speech to this effect: 'This is not my doing though it is on my grounds, but by the subscriptions of myself, the minister and the farmers; and to express gratitude for the harvest; Mr. Andrew requesting it to show you we wish you to be comfortable and well-fed, though not at public houses, and I hope you will not go there.' Then the women and children came outside the tent, and every man was given a third pint of beer.

Sir John opened the pleasure-grounds, and everyone strolled in them. A few played bowls, and Charles, who seemed to enjoy the day, rowed parties in a boat upon the lake. Sir John took Mrs. Andrew and her mother Mrs. Wickes for a promenade, and found Mrs. Andrew very uncomfortable but Mrs. Wickes helped to carry it through, and he hoped the courtesy would do something for the relations between their families. Andrew walked with Lady Catherine, who found him easy. Andrew himself was delighted with her. The conversation was not confined to small talk. They spoke about the difficulty of the doctrine of perseverance, and Andrew believed himself to be penetrating near to her heart, as he could so often penetrate to the heart of a woman. She confessed to him that when she thought she was dying it seemed only like walking from one room to another. 'How mysterious are God's ways!' he meditated. 'A harvest feast brings (us) thus in union after nearly a year's breach.'

He observed that Agnes Boileau, the third daughter, kept cutting him. She had not forgiven him, he knew, for his part in the affair of the coffins, and had avoided speaking to him for nine months. As they walked up and down in the garden, Andrew and Agnes passed and re-passed without speaking. At last he confronted her and offered her his hand. She grasped it warmly, and from that moment all was well again between them.

In the company of Lady Catherine and Agnes, he met Charles Boileau, and heard that he was going to the East and therefore into danger of his life. It was impossible for Andrew not to speak out at such a moment, and he spoke about the peril of Charles' soul. When he spoke seriously to the soul, he spoke with directness and vividness and lack of self-consciousness. Lady Catherine burst into tears, and Sir John came up and led her away. Agnes, left alone with Andrew, thanked him for speaking so to Charles.

Although Andrew believed that he had come so near to Lady Catherine's heart, he remained unaware why his solemn words to Charles had caused such emotion in the Boileau family. He never learnt that Charles, throughout his enjoyment of the festival, was expecting to be arrested on the morrow when he returned to Portsmouth.

On 28th October, Charles met his father for the last time in London. Sir John embraced and kissed his son warmly, 'that if he die soon of disease or war, he may feel a father's forgiveness and love is with him, and if he live, hoping it may win him more to us'.

*   *   *   *   *

On 18th June, 1855, Lord Raglan, the British commander before the forts of Sebastopol in the Crimea, ordered the celebrated and calamitous attack upon the Redan, not because he foresaw anything but failure, but because he felt a duty to support an act of folly committed by the French commander on his right flank. About 4.30 a.m. two columns advanced upon the Redan, each column headed by a hundred men from the Rifles, Lieutenant Charles Boileau amongst them. As his column advanced into the hail of fire from the Redan, Charles suffered a flesh wound in the leg from a Russian bullet. He disregarded it. In the close fighting on the edge of the Redan, a Russian fired at him from point-blank range. The bullet entered his body just below the heart and remained lodged in the hip. He lay on the ground for a time and asked some passing men to carry him back. They were hurrying in retreat and would not stop. Then the cry rose, 'The Russians are coming.' By a great exertion Charles raised himself to his feet, and limped or tottered the two hundred yards to the nearest British trench. They carried him to a field hospital in a tent, and thence, after several days, to the sea. From his hospital bed he wrote to his sister Caroline the last and most sincere and most moving of his many professions of penitence, affirming with conviction that from this date began an entirely new life, and mentioning that a cheque for £40 had been returned. At Balaclava he was put aboard the ship *Great Tasmania*. By the time he reached Constantinople, crude surgery had extracted the bullet and a stream of pus, and he seemed better. Becalmed off Malta, he was suffering from an ulcerated throat and frequent delirium. He was lodged in the palace at Malta built for Napoleon I, which the naval authorities had turned into a hospital, and died there on 1st August, three days after being carried ashore.

News of the severe wound reached Ketteringham by telegraph a week after the assault upon the Redan. Sir John was walking down the avenue with his wife when Huntley leaned out of the window of the study, holding up a letter and calling, 'Here is a note for you, Sir John.' He brought out the cable to them and began saying that the messenger was waiting to be paid. Frightened and angry, Sir John ordered him away; and, sure that Lady Catherine's suspense was equal to his own, opened it on the spot. They read the dispatch together. He got his wife up to her room, brought restoratives for her, and then went to tell the girls.

Before Charles died, they were cheered by two pieces of information which reached them from Sebastopol. Lord Raglan had recommended Charles for gallantry in the fight at the Redan. And what moved the parents even more deeply was the nature of the wound. In the breast pocket of his jacket he had been carrying his prayer book and his mother's miniature. The bullet passed through the prayer book, struck the miniature in one corner, and was thereby deflected towards the hip. It was an infinite comfort to them both to feel that family affection and religion had been his supports to the end.

The letter announcing Charles' death at Malta arrived at Ketteringham on 6th August by the afternoon post. Sir John could not bring himself to tell his wife, and hoped that if he waited until after dinner she would be strengthened by the meal and more able to bear it. After dinner she lay down upon the sofa in the drawing-room and said, 'I fear something. Is all over?' She was in sad hysterics for a time, but they got her to bed and calmed her down. On 18th August, they received their letters back from the Crimea unopened.

For the first time in this history, Sir John asked Andrew to visit him, not from courtesy, but because he sincerely wished for spiritual comfort. Andrew came and thought him much changed, meeker, frightened at his bronchitis, and wanting comfort at his son's death. He was not allowed as long a time of private conversation as he liked. But Lady Catherine hinted that he might sometimes go to read with them. 'Will this ever be?' Andrew asked himself. His hopes rose. 'O that I may

have the meekness of wisdom! I can't think this family have
come hither without some good reason. I prayed much about
the purchaser of Ketteringham.'

Andrew thought that the consolation, which they sought to
derive from the miniature and the prayer book, was pathetic.
The facts ought to be faced. He knew that Charles had not
lived a good life, and felt that he had died a decided enemy to
God. 'Do not dwell upon him,' he told Caroline, the only
member of the Boileau household to whom he might yet speak
on such a theme, and to whom (of all the family except Lady
Catherine) Charles had been closest. 'Leave the matter with
God. No thoughts or anxiety can benefit now.'

*   *   *   *   *

On 11th September, Dr. Innes, the surgeon of the 60th Rifles,
came to stay at Ketteringham. He had known Charles well in
the camp before Sebastopol, where his tent was two away from
Charles' tent, had sailed with him in the *Great Tasmania* and
attended him at Malta. They plied him with questions about
Charles' behaviour during his last few weeks of life. He gave
them the damaged prayer book and miniature, and the fatal
bullet; but he could not satisfy them about the wounded man's
state of mind. They learnt that Charles had not himself been
able to write a letter, and had declined to dictate a letter to his
home. Dr. Innes hinted that Charles had expressed doubt how
he would be received by his father if he reached Portsmouth
alive, and had implied that his behaviour had prevented his
father feeling much affection for him. He talked much of his
mother and of Caroline, and among his last words were an
order to his rough Irish servant, 'Go and stand there and talk
to me about my mother.' He was always cheery, Dr. Innes
said. Did he say anything upon his hospital bed that would
lead them to think of him as penitent? The doctor could not say
that he had heard Charles say anything of the kind. He had not
seemed to like the chaplain at the hospital. Dr. Innes had found
him very reserved. Perforce Sir John was content with the hope
that Charles had felt more than he had publicly expressed, and
let the doctor go, making him a present of Charles' pelisse.

Sir John planned with Mr. Jekell a monument for Charles
in Ketteringham church. Jekell produced a design for a

monument upon a great scale. Sir John shared Andrew's qualms far enough to think this wrong. It was inappropriate that a monument so imposing should commemorate a younger son, and such a younger son, and if all the nine children were to have a memorial so elaborate, there would be no room whatever upon the walls of the chancel. He determined upon a simple little record. He stood inside the church, discussing it with John and Frank, and in the end told Jekell that his admirable design must be made plainer and simpler.

The monument to Charles was erected in Ketteringham church on 20th August, 1856, and there the visitor may still see it upon the north wall. It is a plain and almost unadorned record of Charles' life and death; almost unadorned, for at the base is the simple text, 'Looking to the Captain of his salvation.' Andrew was indignant when he saw the text, and thought it merely untrue. Perhaps he knew nothing of the more elaborate monument which Sir John had rejected. Certainly he was wrong in attributing to Sir John a foolish belief in Charles' salvation. On the contrary, in the recesses of his bedroom Sir John was still tormenting himself whether Charles had died in penitence.

In the village old Mrs. Laud refused to allow a dead branch to be cut from the pear tree in her garden. Charles, when a boy, had been riding the pony Tom Thumb, and had stretched out his hand for a pear. As he held the branch, Tom Thumb had jerked away and left him hanging in mid-air. Mrs. Laud always called it Charles' branch, and would let no one touch it.

X

CAROLINE

From the pulpit in Ketteringham church dropped the words of the preacher, odd and painful, boring and misjudging, but always consistent, decisive, regular, like the dripping of water upon a rock. Servants and housekeepers at the Hall had long been accustomed to partake of the stream. As the eighteen fifties came, even the daughters of the house began to find that this drip of water was not like the chill damp which must be excluded, but contained, for all its strangeness and monotony, the water of life. The power of that pulpit, with the squire's and vicar's pews below, was beginning to affect the hearts of the ladies in the Boileau family.

Andrew had established a restricted, very restricted, communication in things of the spirit with Ama. But Ama was married to the Reverend William Gurney and passed under another's care. Henceforward it was Caroline, the second daughter, who interested Andrew deeply. He liked all three; Ama perhaps with the least confidence at first, but he slowly came to recognize that William Gurney was a man of God; and Ama and Willie sometimes defended him at Ketteringham. Agnes was so kindly and so appreciative, he loved her with a warm affection. But Caroline he liked above all — she was straight and she was honest. If Ama seemed to take after her mother's tenderness, Caroline seemed to share all her father's character and determination. Andrew found himself beginning to admire her.

His dreams, and still more perhaps his wife's, began to imagine alliances. His eldest son, William Wickes Andrew, was a boy of whose industry and intelligence his father had always formed the lowest opinion. He would go up to Caius College, Cambridge, and astound his father by his scholarly prowess. He was a suitable age, not perhaps for Ama but — was it not possible that William Wickes and Agnes, or William Wickes and Caroline, would become united? What an event this would be in the unity of squire and parson . . .

It was not to be. Ama married Mr. Gurney, and in June, 1855, Agnes married the second son of Lord Vernon. But Caroline did not marry. She was no ordinary girl, and no ordinary man could have linked his fate to hers. She was pale, melancholy-seeming, remote, severe, and withal intelligent, clear-headed and decisive. She also has left a diary: in some way the most austere, and the barest, document which comes down from Ketteringham. She wrote her diary that it might be read by others, her sisters; and even her sister Agnes once complained of its dullness. She restricted it to the movement of guests, the weather, the household, the entertainment. Hardly anywhere does she release herself. You can sense the long row of buttons fastened, the high collar and upright spine and sober blouse. The most moving and tragic experience of her life is not mentioned in her own diary, though her record of the bitter days is preserved. If we possessed her diary alone, we should know only that a guest came to the house and spent a few days and toured the district to see the country. We should know nothing at all of the tears, the fascination or the agonies of those few days. Nor should we know anything of those conflicts with her father, inevitable as the strong will of the adult girl encountered the strong will of the parent. Once she wrote in her diary, 'Much trouble . . .' and from another source we know the nature of that trouble. But afterwards she heavily erased the words from the diary, and they can barely be discerned beneath the scribble intended to conceal.

It was not that she lacked a mind, nor that she was uninterested and uninteresting. She was highly educated, could read French and German and Spanish, supervised the books in the library and catalogued them, played upon the piano and the concertian, felt at ease in the London world of political or artistic conversation. More than Ama or her father, she loved the natural beauties of the park at Ketteringham, knew the magic of wild primroses in the woods, the crocuses and snow-drops, dog-violets and cowslips, the sunset glittering pink like the crest of a humming-bird with streaks of lemon below. She watched tenderly over the young lambs in the fields, the peacocks upon the terrace, the swans and ducks upon the lake, the cuckoos and wood-pigeons. She would listen with delight to the pheasants calling in the undergrowth, and be grieved to find the gentlemen shooting those woods next day. Sometimes the reader can almost scent the freshness of the flowers and trees in a Norfolk spring; and he who would know the charm of a Ketteringham childhood a century ago, should turn the pages of Caroline's diary. But there is no art in it, nothing but the record unadorned. In her nature there was no pretentiousness, no façade. Intelligence, determination, and simplicity — the union of these qualities makes a woman formidable.

The diary discloses one unusual element in her growing mind. As she turned into an adult, she became ever more interested in death. Her diary records — with no air of satisfaction nor morbid interest, but more fully than many other matters — the calamities which afflicted persons known to her, even if they were known but faintly. The falling of a tower at Lynn; the fatal disasters then so frequent upon the railways; the naval officer upon Edmund's ship, stabbed in the stomach by a marine; Madame de Vaines, whose gown caught fire while she was undressing and who died in the height of beauty and dissipation; Mr. Pennington's suicide; the man's leg crushed by a wagon — and in the parish, as she visited the parishioners, she encountered death and suffering enough. In January, 1854, Ama's little baby died suddenly and unexpectedly, and Caroline was needed to help her sister. She had loved her Charlie like a mother, and he died in delirium in the Malta hospital.

Death seemed to her imminent and menacing, and she found herself afraid. She had always been a woman of religion. In the fifties (her twenties) the seriousness of life took hold of her spirit. At last she began to know the ministry of Andrew, and to seek Biblical truth from his lips. As the girl grew into a woman, she found herself in that painful predicament of the devout soul, seeking to honour her father and mother, knowing that her father and mother distrusted Andrew, yet convinced that Andrew's ministry was the ministry of the Gospel and ought to be obeyed. In a household where the vicar was hardly welcome, the eldest of the unmarried girls was passing into one of his disciples.

She had begun, like Ama, by sharing her father's opinion of Andrew. She also found relief in the sermons of others when they were in London. She had resented the sermons apparently directed at Boileaus, or the little notes of invitation to the vestry, whereby Andrew sought to assail them individually. In 1846, she was thinking his sermons to be sometimes stupid as well as bad, and she found their length difficult to endure. But she saw more of him and Mrs. Andrew than anyone else in her family. She was the most faithful of the Boileaus in conducting her class of boys in the Sunday School, and she learnt to respect not only Andrew, but Ellen Andrew.

On 22nd February, 1857, she asked Andrew if she might come to see him in the vestry. She had come to say goodbye, as the family was going to London for the season. She said that the upper classes had fewer advantages in religion than others, that she would hear no Gospel sermons in London from poor Mr. Glennie (whose sermons, ten years before, had been such a relief from Andrew's), and asked him to pray for her.

Andrew grasped her hand.

'I have for years,' he said, 'not only pleaded for you but even mentioned your Christian name.'

'Yet do, especially this time,' she said, and went away. Andrew meditated upon it. Once he had less hope of her than of any Boileau, even though she had been less publicly hostile to him about the coffins. He thought that in the vestry there had been a peculiar tenderness and beam upon her countenance which gave him encouragement. He went down upon his knees to plead for her, and in the midst of his prayers resolved to write her anonymous letters upon religious subjects.

The new relationship was sealed in the next year, 1858. She went to consult him about her fear of death. Upon this theme he preached several sermons which comforted her. She asked him not to write letters to her, and not to summon her privately to the vestry, because she could not explain to her parents why she was going. But by December, 1858, she had turned from a parishioner into an adherent. And it was impossible for her to be a faithful disciple of the vicar and a loyal daughter of her own family. Her father, she knew, disapproved of communications with the vicar. She prepared to make her occasions of religious converse at times and places unknown to him. Even her married sisters did not dare to invite Andrew to their houses. In 1858, Caroline and the vicar, unknown to Sir John, were meeting for prayer every Wednesday evening at half-past eight. And under Andrew's ministrations the scrupulous, over-tender, gloomy, introverted temperament came little by little to find peace. He found the absolute integrity of the woman, and could no longer doubt that she was a jewel of God's crown.

She was somehow a link between the vicar and the squire; an unusual link, because the squire resented her converse with the vicar and the vicar was ever afraid that the squire would discover its extent and forbid it. And yet she represented to Andrew something in the Boileau family which drew him, its power and potentiality. She began to take notes of his sermons, and would come to him on Monday to repeat what he had preached. It was inevitable that sooner or later, whatever her sincerity and whatever her tact, her ambiguous relationship between her father and her pastor, already troublesome enough to her sense of loyalty, would be observed in public. It happened over her maid.

In December, 1858, Caroline acquired a new maid, named Mary Ann Taylor. On Sunday, 2nd January, all the family (except Frank who had evidently something on his mind) stayed behind to receive the Sacrament. Mary Ann Taylor had not intended to remain. But moved by a text used in Andrew's sermon ('Why should I be as one that turneth aside from the flocks of thy companions?') she thought 'Why do I turn away?' and stayed with others to receive. Caroline then inquired into her religious upbringing and discovered that her parents were Baptists and that she had never been baptized. On 30th January, Mrs. Badham, the housekeeper, brought Mary Ann into the vestry and asked Andrew to baptize her. Mary Ann confessed that she had slight scruples about the mode of baptism practised in the Church of England and would prefer to be immersed. Andrew at once offered to baptize her, after due preparation, by immersion. In the event it was agreed that she should be baptized by the normal mode in Ketteringham church on Sunday, 20th February.

Five days before the day of baptism, Sir John discovered what had been arranged. He discovered that his wife and even William Gurney knew of the arrangement, but no one had thought it right to inform him. He had a painful talk with his wife, trying to convince her that she had failed in her duty and was much distressed to find that she seemed unaware of any impropriety. At the time of dressing for dinner, a note arrived from Mr. Andrew, to say that he had settled with Mary Ann Taylor to christen her next Sunday and he supposed that Sir John knew of it. The note roused Sir John to grief and anger, and perhaps to a measure of alarm that he would find himself in another controversy with Andrew. After dinner he summoned the maid to his presence. She appeared to him docile, and sorry for having taken such a step without consulting himself or Lady Catherine. She burst into tears; and Sir John said, 'I quite forgive you, and will see what is best to be done.'

He went back to the library and there found his wife and Caroline together. He read them Mr. Andrew's note. Caroline grieved him deeply by saying flatly that nothing had been wrong, and his wife grieved him almost as deeply by showing a disposition to agree. Caroline said that she was sorry; her manner seemed to him an offensive way of saying that she was not. He launched out into a tirade against her stubborn and disrespectful conduct upon this and other occasions; 'I am resolved that you must do otherwise and not set so bad an example to your younger sisters and make us all unhappy by taking so much independence and showing me so little deference or affection; and even now your manner and language is most distressing to me as a parent.'

Caroline softened her manner. Now she expressed her sorrow with evident sincerity.

He calmed down and said, 'That is all I desire. I am sure if you have your eyes open to your faults you will correct them.' He gave her a few more gentle words of reproof and advice, and then kissed her heartily, and sent her away to her room for a short time, and talked a little with his wife.

Next morning he summoned Mary Ann, the maid, once more. She said that she now wished to postpone being christened. He arranged with Lady Catherine that Mrs. Badham should accompany her to Hethersett and give Andrew a note. The note explained that the parents were Baptists and that Sir John was unwilling to sanction her christening till she had communicated with them in London. Mrs. Badham and Mary Ann delivered the note; and Andrew wrote in his diary a comment of peace.

The squire, afraid of controversy with Andrew, asked Mrs. Badham what had happened. He was relieved that it had gone so well. He arranged that Mary Ann should be baptized by Mr. Glennie in London shortly before Easter. She was not immersed.

* * * * *

That March of 1859, the Boileau family went as usual to London for the season, bearing with them a reluctant but dutiful Caroline. Her allegiance to Andrew had not been weakened, but the contrary. Before she went, she seized the opportunity of a meeting in the village to take an hour's walk with him and have out with him the little matters which had seemed to mar his conduct — why had he accepted the sovereign for the removal of the bodies? Had he ever said that Mr. Blomfield, the squire's agent, came home from Norwich drunk? He satisfied her sufficiently, and thought that he had never felt so strong a regard for her.

And so, later in the year, with all the family back at Ketteringham for the winter, the storm began to blow. How to render to God the things that are God's when the commands of Caesar are not the commands of force, but of filial duty and family feeling?

In the Christmas season of 1859, Sir John decided to hold, once again, a dance for his servants, that dance which had caused little Sarah Cooper such qualms a few years before. He had held the dance at the New Year of 1858, and had been pained because Ama and William Gurney absented themselves. He still held, almost defensively now, that dancing was a natural and innocent enjoyment for health and spirits. At Christmas 1859, Caroline thought it wrong to go to the dance. But being a woman of strong mind and character, she had not the weaker resource of Sarah Cooper to avoid a conflict by a measure of diplomacy. Nor had she, like Ama, a husband behind whose defences she could shelter.

She had continued her secret meetings for prayer with Andrew, and met him in the village on their pastoral occasions. One Sunday he found her standing in the pew, waiting for her Sunday school to begin.

She said, 'I expected you would come, and urge me to

decision in speaking to my father plainly about allowing me to decline all worldly company. I feel that I ought, and that I cannot have peace until I do. Yet I feel he would insist, and so make matters worse.'

He did not press her at that moment to decide. But he resolved that one day he would urge it with tenfold earnestness. They went on talking, even to the neglect of her boys in the Sunday school, and as they came out of church after the service she grasped his hand and said with great feeling, 'You won't give me up?'

He said, 'No. The beam on your countenance today cheers me.'

On 27th December, 1859, the squire returned from a ride to Hethersett and round the village. Caroline took her courage in both hands. She came to him and said, 'I feel it so wrong to attend a servants' dance that unless you desire me I had rather not.'

He burst out, 'This is all Mr. Andrew. I forbid you ever to have conversation with him.' He argued with her calmly, but saw that he was making no impression. He consulted Lady Catherine; they agreed that he should speak to her alone and, with every respect for her feeling, tell her that he wished her to be present. He told Caroline that it might otherwise lead 'to an entire derangement of the family — every child and every servant having as much right as you to say they had "a feeling" that some habit or wish of mine as head of the family was wrong and they could not join in it — and so we should become all confusion — and I forfeit my place and the duty God has given me.' But he told her that she had a year's reprieve — for owing to quite other circumstances, trouble among the servants, and New Year's Day, 1860, being a Sunday, he had after all decided not to have a servants' ball that year.

She was touched, put her arms round him and kissed him.

On Sunday, 8th January, at morning service, the peace was broken unwittingly by the vicar. He mounted the pulpit and preached a sermon upon the duties of children towards their parents. What he said is not extant. He almost certainly preached with the needs of Caroline in mind, for he rarely preached without thought for the practical needs of some among his flock. We know from elsewhere that he held the strongest views upon the duty of children to obey their parents in all things lawful. But this was not the impression left by the sermon with Sir John. He summarized it as 'encouraging children to obey God rather than be guided by parents — which meant, Follow me, Mr. Andrew, and not your Father.' He believed that the sermon was aimed to incite Caroline into rebellion.

Then Andrew must have known what had passed between himself and his daughter over the servants' ball? Were the confidences of the house unsafe? Was there secret communication between Andrew and Caroline? He went to his wife. Lady Catherine told him that three or four days before she had learnt from Caroline of meetings with Mr. Andrew in the village. Caroline had told her mother that while the family was away, Andrew had come into the Hall and sat alone with her. Her mother had pointed out how indiscreet this behaviour was, and Caroline had promised to avoid it hereafter.

Sir John was most uneasy. 'How often have I applied to you, almost convinced something of the kind was going on, but have always been met with an assurance I was mistaken; and no watchfulness, or not sufficient watchfulness in consequence of my fears, has been exercised. So that now the evil has got to a great height and I am very apprehensive. I beg you to ascertain also if the maid or Badham privately see Mr. Andrew. It is not unlikely. I know he invited them to the vestry, and formerly some had gone — nominally for religious purposes but it is easily perverted to domestic disturbance.' He would not go out that Sunday evening, but sat alone in his room, with his mind disturbed, reading sermons.

The reprieve was not for a year, but for life. Sir John never again held a servants' ball at Ketteringham, and therefore never needed to insist that his daughter should go. But he had forbidden her to meet Mr. Andrew. She meekly and painfully submitted.

She interpreted the ban with literal strictness. Her father had ordered her to exchange no word with Mr. Andrew and therefore she could not even tell him why she had ceased to meet him. Andrew was puzzled by her behaviour. At first he thought it an accident that their paths failed for so long to cross, that they had no chance of meeting. 'The Lord,' he wrote, 'seems to hinder it, though I know she prays for it.' A few weeks later he was seriously perplexed over it. 'I have tried in vain for weeks to see her but the Lord suffers me not. What can it mean?' On 5th February, he determined to speak to her in church. He went over to her and offered her a handbill. She gave it back and said, 'I think I had better not.' He was pleased that she smiled sweetly at him, as though to assure him that all was well. On 12th February, he tried again while she was waiting in the pew.

She held out her hand, and said, 'Goodbye. I shall not see you again, we are going to town.'

Andrew was about to speak, when she whispered, 'Don't talk to us. Goodbye.'

He could not understand it. 'What can it all mean?' That afternoon Sir John came late to church and found his daughters sitting in their pew with the curtains not drawn across. He stepped forward and violently pulled the curtains together.

Did Sir John suspect that they had held secret meetings? Andrew wondered. When he went out of the church on his way home, she was there, half-hidden by the laurel bush, waiting to give him a goodbye nod. She smiled, and nodded again and again, and disappeared. He took it to be an assurance that he need not be disconcerted about her. 'How will all this end? Is she about to take a stand and declare that she can't again touch the world, for I recommended her to throw herself on her father's affections and ask him to spare her the pain? The mystery however is not pleasant to me. I must look more to the Lord for her; he can bring her feet out of the net. Perhaps Sir John has heard of my spending an hour with her when he was out, or he may have heard of our talks.'

For months the mystery went on. About to meet him in the village street, she would turn tail and disappear. He knew from others that she had great regard for him. 'Is she watched?' he asked himself. He said to Mrs. Haggith, the new school-mistress, not because he believed it but to see what she said, 'I feel Miss Boileau's coldness.'

'O sir,' said Mrs. Haggith, 'Miss Boileau would be vexed if you thought so, for she honours you most highly and stands up for you in public and private.'

He watched with affection Caroline's indefatigable labours for the poor and he worried that she looked so wretchedly ill. He tried to devise means by which he could make her speak to him. Like any young lover, he determined to see whether neglect would effect change in her. He would be obvious in avoiding her. Now he was the one who, ostentatiously, turned aside if he saw her coming down the street. Not until two years after Sir John had decreed the ban did Andrew receive reliable news why Caroline was thus behaving.

He first heard the news from a friendly vicar. And in the end, so he imagined, his studied neglect forced her into speaking. One Sunday in 1863, between the services, he was sitting inside the reading-desk, looking over the skeleton of his sermon for the afternoon. She ascended the steps and addressed him.

'You ought not to distrust me,' said Andrew.

'I have been forbidden to speak to you, and I had promised. I hope God is bringing matters about.' She added, 'It is not distrust of you, but myself. I must go. I am afraid I may be tempted to talk with you.'

They met next day, out in the parish near Easton's. She did not look at him.

'Face me,' said Andrew. 'Don't shun me. You ought to have told me a long time ago.'

'I had not an opportunity.' She seemed at last ready to talk.

'I suppose this will be the last time of saying goodbye.' The family was departing again to the London season.

'Don't forget me,' said Andrew. They shook hands. It seemed to him that her hand lingered in his.

He deceived himself by imagining that his stratagem of neglect had won her. 'I have caught her with guile,' he thought. It was a misinterpretation, characteristic of his unsubtle knowledge of human behaviour. Circumstances outside the control of Andrew had been leading Caroline to the hope that the ban might be lifted, or at least that a disregard of it would not be disloyal.

*   *   *   *   *

Sir John had been worrying about Caroline as much as Andrew, but for different reasons. It puzzled him that so intelligent and coherent a girl should be open to the influence of a man so unworthy or so unfitted to be the guide of her soul.

'It is wonderful the influence so injudicious and inconsisent and often untrue a man possesses over such educated young females — as well as over the poor.' Perhaps, he thought, with an attempt at psychological diagnosis unusual for him, it is because she dislikes parental control and finds that a belief in the authority of religion or of the minister justifies her in dissent or opposition. Perhaps, he thought, it is because she is a spinster; and her behaviour is the natural result of strong feelings and impulses undeveloped by marriage and children and finding their outlet in religious fervour. It was true that she was showing no signs whatever of wishing to be married.

She had not lacked suitors. As long ago as 1850, Mr. Fletcher, the school inspector, had asked her father for her hand. Sir John had told him that his girls could not be happy if they were to marry out of their habits of life. He had informed her of the proposal, and to his satisfaction she distinctly and quietly and calmly declared against Mr. Fletcher. In 1858, there was a Dr. Guggenbuhl, who seemed to attempt to excite her through her charitable feelings, but Sir John was soon rid of him. By 1859, the village of Ketteringham was beginning to comment that she did not marry. The old cottagers would sometimes be blunt. Blind old Cooper silently felt her finger and said, 'Tis not here, Miss!'

'No,' said Caroline, 'not a ring of the kind you mean.'

Andrew wondered if being a spinster was a trial to her. He once told her that he was praying for her to meet a godly husband. Caroline continued to seek permission to avoid those places where eligible husbands, whether godly or ungodly, were to be found.

In July, 1863, a suitor, both eligible and godly, appeared at Ketteringham.

Mr. Anthony Thorold was an evangelical clergyman, well known in London as the rector of St. Giles'-in-the-Fields. He had been married before, but his wife had died tragically. He was thirty-eight years old and a coming man, indeed a future bishop successively of Rochester and Winchester. They had met him in the London season of 1863. He arrived to stay at Ketteringham on 7th July and remained as a guest until the 16th. He inspected the village school, paid various calls in the company of Caroline and her sister Theresa, attended Mr.

Andrew's tea and bazaar for the Jews and missionaries ('Wondrous thing!' thought Andrew, seeing Sir John arrive with two carriages full, 'when I think in twenty-two years he has never before crossed my lawn — what hath God wrought!'), visited the hall at Tacolneston, worshipped in Ketteringham church, heard Mr. Andrew preach upon election and agreed with Sir John that some of the language was perilous, sang religious music to the company after dinner and won the devotion of the girls, and made a sight-seeing trip to the church at Wymondham and to Caistor Camp, where a labourer gave them a coin of the Emperor Constantius.

After dinner on the day when they came back from Wymondham, Caroline brought out the croquet hoops and mallets and began to set them up on the bowling green. Sir John was suddenly indignant. It might spoil the bowling green; why not the front lawn? And should she not have asked him before bringing out the croquet set? He called to her. She took no notice. He called again. She seemed not to listen, but to be engaged in laughing at one of the gentlemen who was trying on a lady's bonnet at the other end of the terrace.

Sir John caught her by the arm.

'But Carry, answer me when I speak to you.'

'I did not hear.'

He was vexed that she made no apology and looked injured.

'But you ought. I wanted to tell you it is better to put the croquet on the lawn which I had already good humouredly settled with Lucy and one of the younger ones.'

'I knew nothing of it, and had nothing to do with it.'

'You act as mistress and wish to be so in all things and therefore I must look to you for these things.'

She turned round with an injured air, as though to supplicate the company for protection. He turned to Thorold and walked away with him, hoping that he had not heard the discord, and discussing with him a father's difficulty in managing three grown-up daughters who had had their own way, being indulged by a gentle mother; and then his sensitive, heated mind passed to tell Thorold about the boys — Charles dead, and John dead, and Edmund lost to the family, and only Frank remaining. It was an odd conversation for a father with a man who, as he had an inkling, might be his son-in-law. Yet Mr. Thorold was so mild, he was so true a friend, that Sir John felt himself rushing onwards for the sake of advice. Thorold found that he had little enough to say.

Thorold left Ketteringham on 16th July; and soon it was being rumoured through the Hall that he and Caroline were to be engaged. They had been seen to go walking together every day, and Caroline was now observed to be depressed and in low spirits. Her father tried to caress her, and cheer her up. After a few days he could not bear the suspense of not knowing what had happened. The form of his question showed what he feared. He asked her, 'Did you tell Mr. Thorold that you do not mean to marry?'

He got no answer but grief touched with hysteria. He therefore took to writing her letters, and received coherent letters from her in reply. Mr. Thorold had indeed proposed marriage to her and she had refused. Both of them had been wretched afterwards. Sir John hoped that she would be sustained by a woman's pride and gratification 'at having been asked by a worthy, able and honourable man — approved by her parents and family — especially at her age, when marriage is less likely'. But this kind of gratification did not come easily to Caroline's breast. She pitied Mr. Thorold and was distressed when she found that he believed himself to have been refused because he had proposed in a manner imperfect or cold. She asked her father to make it clear to Mr. Thorold that her refusal was nothing to do with the manner of the proposal; that she did not mean, perhaps that she did not think it right, to marry. She told her father that she belonged to God.

And so Mr. Thorold turned away, and found another wife, and mounted that ladder which in the end would lead him to two bishoprics. And Caroline turned finally towards the single life and the ministries which the single life made possible — relieving the destitute, visiting the sick, teaching the young; and carried with her the two youngest sisters, Mary and Theresa, into renunciation of the world. In a flash of insight she once confessed, 'I give up the world, not in faith, but because I never cared about it!' In another religious tradition she would have been a nun, indeed an abbess. When Sir John made his will, he inserted a provision that his three unmarried daughters should not receive a dowry upon marriage unless that marriage was approved by Dr. Pelham, the bishop of Norwich. None of them would ever have wished or needed to ask Dr. Pelham for his approval, even if Sir John's codicil had not rescinded the effect of the clause.

*   *   *   *   *

The relations between Caroline and Andrew were changed by the death of Lady Catherine.

In the autumn of 1861, John Boileau, the heir, died at Dieppe after his long illness. On 13th January, 1862, cancer was diagnosed in Lady Catherine's breast, and her future was pronounced hopeless. She dragged out her life for unexpectedly long months of 1862, with Caroline as the nurse and even watchdog of the sick-room, warding off visitors, sleeping with her mother at nights, superintending her meals and her washing.

Andrew's opinion of Sir John was such that he did not think him to care about Lady Catherine. That lady, with the lovely dark hair and the serene, submissive face, had seemed to the parish to be subject to her powerful husband. In public he was the master, and his sense of propriety would probably have forbidden him to allow tenderness to appear before the world. But Andrew was altogether mistaken. Lady Catherine, though submissive, was less submissive in her bedroom than before the public eye. And Sir John, though decorous and perhaps formal before the public eye, had given his heart to his wife. Her long illness had been a perpetual source of grief and worry to him. Day after day he would think of her health, and hope, and plan, and consult doctors, and discuss whether to go abroad, or to Brighton, or to Tunbridge Wells, be cast down by her bad times and be cheered by her good times. When she was gone it seemed to him that Ketteringham Hall was a solitude. He wandered through its rooms grieving at their emptiness.

As the long agonies of the death-bed took their terrible course, he felt the need for consolation of the spirit. He could not readily think of Andrew in the light of a comforter. As late as 1860, they had conducted the last of the quarrels of Ketteringham church, a quarrel whether the vicar had the right to put seats for strangers in the aisle.[1] Sir John received consolation from his son-in-law Willie Gurney whenever he was staying in the house. Andrew once asked the bishop, Dr. Pelham, to vis him. But now, at last, Sir John began to turn to Andrew — reluctantly, with nerves alert, with suspicion in the mind, but still to Andrew. He would stop Andrew in the parish to converse with him, he allowed him to begin visiting the Hall regularly, so that they might converse and pray together. 'Surely his eyes are opening,' said Andrew. They talked of the good life, of the dangers of high society, of the wrongness of sporting clergymen, of how to conquer those fits of passion to which Sir John said he was liable, a confession to which Andrew did not demur. 'I have urged him to forget the past and begin to serve the Lord.' They talked of the inmost secrets of the family. For the first time Andrew was brought into the Boileau confidence over Edmund. He felt himself encouraged in all these visits by the hope that Caroline was praying for them in the room overhead. 'I need much wisdom just now in dealing with this man.'

Sir John was tried sometimes by the length, and sometimes by the enthusiasm, of Andrew's visits. He suspected that new presbyter was but old priest, and was afraid that his minister might try to secure a priestly dominance over his soul. He thought that Andrew's suggestion of prayer at a common time for Edmund was 'a getting in of the small end of the wedge to bring me under his directions', and when Andrew preached on Sunday that man ought not to complain if he had an unrighteous son (did he mean Edmund?), Sir John thought that such a sermon made it difficult to accept his spiritual assistance. 'It has so much more the impression of seeking to be important and

---

[1] Andrew put benches in the chancel aisle for a family of strangers. Blomfield removed them to the vestry. Andrew put them back in the chancel. Letters passed to and fro between the bishop, Sir John, Blomfield, and Andrew — one letter of Andrew's was twenty pages long. Blomfield not merely removed the benches a second time but put them in a cart and deposited them at Andrew's house. Andrew ordered them back to the church to be placed inside his own pew: 'Surely Sir John will not turn them out of my pew, but I must only yield step by step as compelled.' The battle was finally lost when Mrs. Andrew called Blomfield to his face Sir John's 'catspaw', and both the Andrews felt constrained to apologize.

priestly than a comforting brother-Christian . . . I cannot make him a guide or a director.' He would be moved by these occasions to anger. He was as critical as ever of the sermons from the pulpit. And he observed in their private conversations those faults to which he had always objected in the pulpit — the want of judgment, the joyous irrationality, the vanity of the man who kept harping upon all that God had used him to do. He tried to make allowances; he admired the clarity of his grasp of Scripture, and his burning sincerity; but the clarity was such that he wrested every discussion towards his own view, and failed to catch another's point of view. 'Though we talk pleasantly and with mutual respect,' wrote Sir John, 'I do not feel much enlightened or soothed by our talks.'

In one of their conversations, they discussed their differences, in an atmosphere far different from all previous discussions. Andrew asked at the end if they might pray about them. Sir John assented but said that they should go to his room, lest they should be interrupted. As they went, Caroline passed through the dining-room. Sir John beckoned Andrew into the library, and Caroline followed. Andrew hesitated — should he notice her? Would it force her to break her father's order? She came forward and said to Sir John, 'Papa, I am going just to shake hands with Mr. Andrew before the service.'

Andrew took her (coolly, he thought) by the hand. Sir John asked Andrew to go with him into Lady Catherine's room. It was the first time that the widower had entered that room since his wife died. Andrew said prayers; and then Sir John added a prayer that they might live in peace, and they walked together to the church for the afternoon service. Someone stopped Sir John to speak to him; and so Andrew was left alone, and Caroline followed him into the vestry.

She said, 'My mamma, before dying, left this special message: Tell Mr. Andrew, I die relying on the merits of Jesus Christ.'

Lady Catherine too, then? He knew that Caroline had long been his disciple, that her younger sisters Theresa and Mary had lately become so, that the housekeeper and the maid, like so many of their predecessors, hung upon his words. And now Lady Catherine. 'How will all this end?' he asked himself. He wished that something could have happened among the menfolk of the Boileau family. Charles, he was almost sure, had died without religion. John had died, he knew not in what state of mind. Frank was pleasant and friendly, would he be more? Edmund was a son in a far country; was it possible that he might return like the prodigal? And Sir John himself — was it possible that at last the daily breastplate of prayer for him was receiving an answer?

To Lady Catherine's memory Sir John founded the Catherine ward at the Norwich hospital, and a Catherine convalescent home at Lowestoft. To her memory he decided to insert a stained-glass window to St. Catherine in Ketteringham church. It was to be placed in the little window by the side of his pew.

On Monday, 12th January, 1863, he and the designer, Mr. Jekell, met Andrew at Ketteringham church. It was symptomatic of the new relationship that Andrew was invited to attend the discussion — he had never before been invited to discuss the squire's monuments. Sir John thought that Andrew might object to the plan; he was pleased to find that the opposition was mild. Andrew at first seemed to dislike the idea of a *saint* in the window and suggested an *apostle* instead; but afterwards he seemed to talk about it with Jekell as a natural thing. On the Wednesday, Mr. King came and put up a little sketch of St. Catherine in the window, and after breakfast Sir John took his three girls out to see it. They said that they admired it but . . . Mary and Theresa thought that people might cavil at it. Caroline said, 'Though I can give no reason for it, I have a feeling against it.' She said that the people would believe it to represent the Virgin Mary. Sir John, the new Sir John, gave way. 'I therefore can no longer wish it — much as the idea has pleased myself — to do that which is against Mr. Andrew's wish, I think, and also my daughters.'

That June, 1863, upon the first anniversary of his wife's death, Andrew offered to visit him and his daughters. It was raining in the morning, but in the afternoon Sir John was able to walk out with the girls, one by one, until half-past five, when Andrew came. He was invited into the drawing-room, and asked to pray not only with Sir John, but with the three girls. Were the barriers finally down, wondered Andrew? He was able to have a private word with Caroline. She told him that she was now permitted to talk with him on spiritual subjects provided she did not talk with him about the state of her own soul. She told him that she had said to her father, 'I cannot promise not to speak to Mr. Andrew of divine things if he speaks to me.'

When Andrew returned home, he wrote Sir John a letter which has not survived. As may be expected, the contents of the letter were not drafted with prudence. Sir John thought it a foolish, injudicious, mistaken letter, and all his defences rose again. He showed his brother the letter, and his brother said that it was a great impertinence. Sir John did not think that it was impertinent. 'I believe it only excessive vanity and desire to bring everybody spiritually under — and as himself something better than his neighbours and a manifestly saved soul.' His critical faculty was not dormant. When Andrew's sermons offended him (which was not infrequently), he still tore them in shreds in his diary. Perhaps he was inclined to add to the condemnation more allowance than formerly. 'To evening church and very hot and very long sermon. General Boileau and Charles [Sir John's brother] both expressed their weariness and discomfort at it and Mr. Andrew's manner. But the people all are attentive and like it and that is the great thing and come readily to church and look to their Bibles — so any discomfort to myself or those who, blessed with education, may divert themselves with prayer, is not to be dwelt upon' (12th July, 1863).

Sir John was beginning to decline now, to age rapidly. His cough was troublesome, and his stomach; he was nearly toothless; he was growing deaf; he found an altogether new capacity for going to sleep during the sermons at evening prayer; he found tears rising quickly to the surface when he thought of his gentle wife, and irritation rising even more quickly when he felt his daughters to be disrespectful towards him or inconsiderate.

He was still able to read to the Archaeological Society a paper on 'Reaping machines as known to the Romans'. He much enjoyed an archaeologizing tour to Scotland in 1864. In 1865, he helped Bishop Pelham to prevent the church congress at Norwich from disintegrating between the tugs of ecclesiastical partisans, among whom he numbered Andrew. He was vigorous enough to be difficult with his doctors. And in a crisis, he could still act with the old decision, the old courage.

On 8th December, 1864, he was at breakfast with the girls. Looking out of the window, they saw the labourer, Brightwen, leading out the little Brittany bull, apparently in a playful mood, to his tether. One of the girls cried, 'Oh! he has got him down and is goring him.' Sir John jumped up, ran to the window and saw the bull goring Brightwen. He threw up the window, leaped out and ran across the grass. Caroline leaped out after him and ran behind, until he sharply ordered her back to the house, alarmed for her safety. He ran up to the wounded man lying on the ground. His arrival distracted the bull from making another push at Brightwen. They watched each other tensely, a few feet apart; and then, still watching the bull, Sir John stooped down and released Brightwen's arm, which was caught in the picketing chain that had been used to lead the bull. Then he rose and took his stance between Brightwen's body and the bull; and there they stood facing each other, warily, until the butler and the workmen and the stable keeper and the flyman arrived. Sir John still stood guard while the men fetched a chair and carried Brightwen away on it through the stable gate, and someone fetched a cow to soothe the bull.

It was no mean act of courage for a man in his seventy-first year. Brightwen's wound in the belly proved to be mortal, and he died in Norwich hospital five weeks later. Sir John visited him in hospital, and Andrew conducted his funeral.

They were not altogether a happy expectation of death, those last few years. It was a great consolation to him that Frank made an excellent marriage with Lucy Nugent and came to live at Tacolneston, and was soon prominent in the county. But he himself was becoming dependent upon his three unmarried daughters, and a man who had been accustomed to organize the footmen and the butler found it difficult to see others organizing them differently. Moreover, his daughters were not always harmonious. Mary and Theresa found Caroline a mistress inclined to be tyrannical or possessive, Caroline seemed sometimes to resent the intrusions or conduct of her younger sisters; to believe that Mr. Andrew was her private clergyman and her sisters should have no close friendship with him. Sir John lay at the mercy of these feminine gusts. He could not help a wistfulness, a looking back to the great days of Ketteringham hospitality, the days when Guizot and Hallam and Stanley and

Lord John Russell had been royally entertained and had charmed the company with their wit and information. He could not help contrasting the idyll of his marriage with the little vexations of companionship with three resolute daughters.

He saw that he could no longer influence the girls. He attempted to stop them from visiting, unchaperoned and un-protected, slums and hospitals and workhouses, but the attempt was fruitless. He occasionally came into conflict with Caroline over singular scruples — once over a letter which he asked her to write on a Saturday, and which she at first refused to write because it would go on Sunday. But for the most part he sub-mitted. As early as February, 1863, he had given up receiving any guests (except family and intimates) on a Sunday because Caroline said that it was wrong.

The squire's new gentleness and devotion seemed to Andrew a˜wonderful thing; a conversion. He wrote in his diary (1863), 'Sir John chairman at Bible meeting and spoke admirably and to the point. All the Boileaus there! £4 3s. 6d. He marvellously governs his temper, but sometimes he is overcome but I feel sure, 'tis a pang to him.' (1864), 'Thanks to God for Sir John's change of conduct even though there be no change of heart, but I despair not of that. He has been so kind in sending Ellen game and making many enquiries; and the other day he sent through Mary to say he had brought a scarlet cloak for Ellen Laura [Andrew's eldest daughter] if she would accept it. Of course as a clergyman I could not have my daughter so dressed, and my dear child was soon convinced, and therefore a beauti-ful ermine muff was sent instead . . .' (1866), 'Sir John wonder-fully changed, listens attentively and is becoming evangelical in principle, and ready to aid societies; very fond of my dear Lucy and Ellen and so kind if any of us are ill.'

With Sir John the battle was over. Under Andrew's instruc-tion he began to re-organize his life of prayer, and his efforts to cure fits of anger. The books of divinity which he read were no longer those of which Andrew disapproved. He gave up reading Charles Kingsley and began to read the evangelical Roberts of Wood Rising. He gave up Trench on the Parables, in which he found no food for the soul, and began to read Thomas Scott. He learnt Andrew's way of preparing the soul to meet death. All the barriers on ministry to the girls were down. He had succumbed, in some part to the courage, the integrity, and the perseverance of the vicar with whom he still partly disagreed — but still more to the insistent cry of the human soul, in the end, for the consolation of the spirit.

But his last comment upon a sermon of Andrew ought to be recorded (29th August, 1868), 'To church but quite knocked up with its length and the long rambling sermon . . .' And later in the same day, 'Scolded Peel of Wymondham Common, a favourite of Mr. Andrew, — ill conditioned fellow.'

EPILOGUE

THE two men aged; but Andrew was nine years younger and his wirier constitution enabled him to outlive Sir John for many years. In the autumn of 1868, Sir John, struggling for health, removed himself and his two younger daughters to Torquay, and died there in the spring of 1869. The funeral was at Ketteringham, and though Bishop Pelham came out to conduct the service, Andrew preached the sermon. Afterwards he asked the bishop's permission to ride in his carriage part of the way to Norwich. He wanted to consult him on what to do with the new squire, once Sir John's son Frank, now transformed into Sir Francis. He mentioned to the bishop the long history of his trials with Sir John. The bishop said, 'You have had a great recompense in your labours in that house.'

In his will, Sir John left £1,000 to construct an ornamental drinking fountain at the junction of the Newmarket and Ipswich roads into Norwich. A fine group, with a mother quenching the thirst of her child, was designed by Boehm and duly erected in 1874; and there it now stands, with hundreds of motorists hourly passing, the most familiar and most unheeded of all the monuments of Sir John Boileau. Boehm's plaster cast, pure and tranquil and meek in its whiteness, is said to have been taken from a likeness of Lady Catherine, and now stands fittingly in the kindergarten at Ketteringham.

The three unmarried girls were left to fend for themselves. Theresa died in 1872, leaving one of Andrew's grandchildren, who was her godson, £50 in her will. Mary lived on at Torquay, full of goodness and charity and labour for the poor. Caroline, just after her father's funeral, told Andrew that she wanted to be a nurse. But three years later she had become a travelling preacher, journeying round the country with the Methodist minister, Mr. Reed. She preached to the holiday-makers upon the beach at Saltburn; she spent long hours in lonely prayer; she led prayer meetings every day, and ministered to the dying and the drunken; she climbed high upon the rocks at Tunbridge Wells and preached a sermon to a crowd of rough lads upon the common below; she sang hymns in London Street, Hoxton; she gave tea parties to fallen girls; she preached in the centre of the old market at Hastings, where the laundresses would not gather round, but looked out of their windows at her or sat upon the sills to listen; she used the Temperance Hall at Hastings on several Sunday evenings; she preached at Liverpool standing on a chair in Duckingfield. On 19th June, 1873, she even visited Ketteringham with Mr. Reed, and held a great evangelistic meeting in the Hall, about 250 persons coming from the villages to hear. 'What a blessing,' she wrote, 'to have the Hall used for such a purpose!' Mr. Andrew was not able, or did not think it right, to attend this meeting.

But soon disease found her and held her. After a lingering illness she died at Bryanstone House in Harrogate, on 2nd April, 1877, from the effects of an operation. Andrew preached the funeral sermon on a text which moved her soul nineteen years before, and the bishop came over to bury her. They sang in the church a hymn of her own composing — 'Have I chosen Jesus?' She was forty-eight years old.

Sir Francis came to Ketteringham and lived there for a time. Though he was regarded by Andrew as impetuous and imperious, he was never allowed to be like his father in having his entire way about the church; and he set a good example to the parishioners, in spite of an unfortunate habit of drawing pictures in his prayer book during the sermon. While the church was being cleaned, he allowed the services to be held in the great hall, with the proviso that strangers should not be admitted. But in 1881, disliking Ketteringham or finding it expensive, he let it to a member of Parliament named Captain Price.

On 28th February, 1881, there was a disaster in the pulpit. Andrew lost the thread in his sermon, preached at very great length and with such repetitions as to alarm his wife so that she left the church; he noticed her going out but thought she was unwell. It was the first sign that he would not be fit much longer to preach his two sermons every Sunday. He began to be retrospective, nostalgic, autobiographical; childhood and youth began to appear in brighter colours than the recent past; his grandchildren loomed larger to him than his children. He remembered how a servant poured scalding milk down his back as he ran along a passage, and the skin peeled off with the shirt; how with a pea-shooter he had shot pellets of paper, containing the answers, to a friend in the examination room at Oxford; how he had cowered behind in the cart as his drunken father flogged a new horse down the hill near Boughton until he leapt out in terror, picked himself up bruised, and found his father lying in the road; how as a child he had wished to grow his hair in a little topknot like Mrs. Burnaby, who lived in a pretty cottage nearby and always kept plum cake for him on his return from school, and how he cried because his topknot refused to stand erect; how he took his bow and arrows, and shot down the hens which trespassed in his garden; how he played hide-and-seek and triumphed by hiding in the top curtain of a fourposter bed; how he carried the lamp for his drunken schoolmaster two miles upon a dark night until the schoolmaster collapsed over a heap of stones; how Tinker Wells had tried to bully him at school ... the memories came crowding round, warming him as his friends died one by one and left him solitary in his generation. He thought that the modern evangelicals did not equal the giants of the past.

In February, 1887, he found that in odd moments he could not speak.

On Easter Sunday he preached as usual in Ketteringham. On Easter Monday, as it was Bank Holiday, several of his Norwich friends came for the day; and he exerted himself too much. On Tuesday, 12th April, he suffered a stroke while in the garden and found that again he could not speak. He was put to bed, with a mind calm but not clear, and was unable to make himself understood. He knew that he could not preach at Ketteringham again, and therefore resigned the living; he had to be assisted to sign the deed of resignation. On 1st June, 1887, Ellen and he left Wood Hall and began to live at Stoneleigh House at Sawbridgeworth. He was not allowed to read or write and spent his time gardening. He did not hanker after Ketteringham. He thought that to be among his people and yet unable to minister to them would be more than he could bear, and so he was resigned and happy to be away. He was glad to hear that his successor preached the Gospel faithfully, amused to hear that henceforth he would live within the parish of Ketteringham and so 'Sir Francis will have all his own way'. He found Sawbridgeworth to be a barren land, a wild and howling wilderness, for no faithful preaching was to be found. Sometimes he would go out to High Wych, or to the chapel, in search of the Gospel. But, although with pain, he followed the choral services at the parish church and winced under the intoning and the speed with which the prayers were read; and even attended the curate's lectures upon Shakespeare which he thought an unsuitable subject for a minister of the Gospel and incidentally poor lectures, but which he attended lest he be thought precise and that he might know the people and perhaps find a chance of speaking a word of truth. And so the stern and gentle mind slipped quietly down, first into blankness, and then into death. The last entry in the diary was made on 29th June, 1889. He died on 21st November, 1889, and was buried in the church-yard at Ketteringham, not far from the mausoleum where Sir John lay, the mausoleum for which he had received so reluctant a fee of twenty-five pounds.

Sources

SIR JOHN BOILEAU's diary is deposited through the Norfolk Record Society in the Norwich public library, with other papers preserved from Ketteringham. The diary begins in 1839, when he left England for his continental tour, and ends in February, 1869, a month before his death. There are certain sections missing — especially 1846-1850, which, however, is still extant and in private hands; and two other short sections were probably destroyed for personal reasons, as one of them contains the day of his wife's death.

In private hands are Ama Boileau's fragmentary diary, Caroline's diary, Caroline's collection of letters about Charles, a number of Owen Stanley's letters, and Lady Catherine's fragments. So are Andrew's diary and Archdeacon Philpot's autobiographical journal.

Andrew's diary is contained in two big volumes, the first from his ordination to 1855, the second from 1855 to his last illness. Unlike Sir John Boileau, he was not regular nor disciplined in daily writing; he wrote when he felt moved to write. Far the fullest years of writing are 1839-1847; after 1848, he was much more irregular and occasionally left the book unused for months on end.

In private hands is an album of records kept at Ketteringham Hall for all the members of the family to write comments.

The records of Ketteringham church are in exceptionally good condition, because of Sir John's dictatorial iron chest, and because Sir Raymond Boileau took a remarkable and scholarly interest in them.

There are interesting glimpses of later Ketteringham in one or two of Ethel Boileau's novels, especially *Turnip Tops* (Hutchinson).

Index

All Futura Books are available at your bookshop or newsagent, or can be ordered from the following address:
Futura Books, Cash Sales Department,
P.O. Box 11, Falmouth, Cornwall.

Please send cheque or postal order (no currency), and allow 45p for postage and packing for the first book plus 20p for the second book and 14p for each additional book ordered up to a maximum charge of £1.63 in U.K.

Customers in Eire and B.F.P.O. please allow 45p for the first book, 20p for the second book plus 14p per copy for the next 7 books, thereafter 8p per book.

Overseas customers please allow 75p for postage and packing for the first book and 21p per copy for each additional book.